GAMES OF THE
AMERICAN
INDIAN

Hopi Indian dolls and toys made of clay.

GORDON C. BALDWIN

GAMES OF THE AMERICAN INDIAN

Illustrated with photographs

W • W • Norton & Company • Inc.
New York

*The photographs on pages 11, 45, 54, and 56,
courtesy Gordon C. Baldwin.*

TO THE TUCSON JUVENILE WRITERS GANG:

*Betty Baker, Florence Laughlin,
Betty Hubka, and Wayne Doughty,
with special thanks to Betty Baker
for the idea that led to this book.*

ACKNOWLEDGMENTS

I should like to express my thanks and appreciation to the following individuals and institutions for their cooperation in providing many of the illustrations for this book:

Dr. Thomas Cain, Director, Heard Museum, Phoenix; Mrs. Margaret C. Blaker, Archivist, Office of Anthropology, Smithsonian Institution; Wilma Kaemlein, Arizona State Museum; Nancy Peabody, American Museum of Natural History; and Mr. William Neil Smith, Tucson.

The illustrations of string figures in Chapter 9 have been reproduced from Stewart Culin's *Games of the North American Indians,* 24th Annual Report of the Bureau of American Ethnology, Smithsonian Institution, Washington, 1907, and from Caroline Furness Jayne's *String Figures and How to Make Them,* Charles Scribner's Sons, 1906 (reprinted by Dover Publications, 1962).

The line drawings on pages 29, 32, 34, 36, 62, 64, 66, 68, 69, 75, 77, 80, 86, 87, 88, 89, 94, 98, and 102 are also reproduced from Culin's *Games of the North American Indians.*

CONTENTS

LIST OF ILLUSTRATIONS

INTRODUCTION

Cries that were similar to, "Play ball" and "Button, button, who's got the button?" echoed throughout most of North America hundreds of years before Christopher Columbus set sail on his historic voyage of discovery.

But nobody shouted "Let's play cowboys-and-Indians." There were thousands of Indians around, but there were no cowboys and no horses or cows.

Most popular books picture the noble "Redman" as a haughty, poker-faced individual who rarely cracks a smile and even more rarely laughs out loud. Actually,

Indians can be solemn and dignified, when the occasion demands, as it generally does during ceremonies or in the presence of strangers. But Indians, by nature, are a long way from being morose and sober-faced. They have a good sense of humor and like to joke and laugh and have a good time. In fact, most of them not only have their mother-in-law jokes but also their father-in-law jokes as well.

Indian boys and girls might be brought up to be "quiet as mice" in the company of their elders or of strangers. But whenever they could, they played with toys and games just like boys and girls of today. And, if you could watch Indian youngsters playing the ring-and-pin or the hoop-and-pole game, as I have, you would never again call Indians grave or reserved. They were as excited and noisy as any crowd at a high school basketball or football game.

Indian life five hundred to a thousand years ago wasn't easy. Yet, like most of us, the Indians weren't content with a humdrum existence. They still found time for play and recreation.

Like the games of most other primitive peoples, Indian games were not played merely for amusement. Many were games of chance, often played for high stakes. Many games were closely tied in with ceremonies and rituals and could only be played at certain times of the year. Some games might bring rain for crops or game animals to hunters or cure sickness or frighten away evil spirits or, as some Indians believed, even keep the sun and moon moving in their proper places.

There was also a link between myths and legends and games. Many Indian tribes have legends in which a supernatural being, a culture hero as he is often called, defeats human contestants in games of skill, speed, cunning, or magic. The Pueblo Indians of Arizona and New Mexico, for example, thought that their hoop-and-pole game was connected with their War Gods and, thus, women were never permitted to play that game. Similarly, the Navaho Indians say that their ancestors were taught to play string games by the ancient Spider people, which accounts for the web-like patterns that you find in this game.

It is often difficult to tell just how old a toy or game is since archaeologists can't dig up games as easily as they can pots and pans and houses. Sometimes all we can say about a particular toy or game is that, to the best of our knowledge, we think it is aboriginal (meaning that it was first used or invented or discovered by the American Indians themselves).

Though they didn't play such games as cowboys-and-Indians or cops-and-robbers, they seem to have had similar hunt-and-chase games.

Naturally Indian children did not have the wide range of toys and games available to today's youngsters in drug stores, department stores and supermarkets. Monopoly, Sorry, Clue, Scrabble and Checkers were unknown to them. So were electric train sets, electric football, baseball and ice-hockey games. They had never heard about or seen tricycles, bicycles, red wagons or rocking horses. Today children are amused and entertained by ant farms, complete with live ants. To city children who have never seen an ant this might be a lot of fun. But it would have had very little appeal to most Indian children living next door to millions of ants.

Indian children made their own toys and games or had their fathers and mothers or older brothers and sisters make them. And they used whatever was handy —sticks, stones, bark, leaves, grass, reeds, shells, animal skins, berries, nuts, seeds, feathers, branches, squash, gourds, animal and bird bones, corncobs and corn-husks.

Many of their games were similar to those still being played today—hide-and-seek, tag, follow-the-leader, blind-man's buff, button, button, various kinds of ball games, guessing games, playing house, and hunting and warfare games.

In some ways, toys and games haven't changed greatly during the past few thousand years. To a child, toys and games are playthings, things to have fun with. To parents, they are usually thought of as things to keep children amused and out of mischief for a few hours. Today, we have added what we call educational toys, toys that teach children to learn by doing. Yet educational toys aren't new. Instruction through play was common in most American Indian nurseries: some of their play was pure fun, but a lot was practice for future warfare, hunting, farming and keeping house.

Playing with toys and games was, and still is, an important part of growing up. Many of us still haven't grown up. What boy hasn't discovered that his father wants equal playing rights to the new electric train that the boy thought was his own birthday present. Since most Indian toys and games were merely cut-down versions of simple adult utensils and games, it was probably a lot easier for an Indian parent of five hundred years ago to resist the urge to get down on the floor and play with his youngster's new toy or game.

Before we go any further we should discuss the physical stereotyping of the Indian. There isn't now and there never was a typical American Indian, just as there is no typical American today. Indians can be tall or short, skinny or fat, long-headed, broad-headed or medium-headed, broad-faced or narrow-faced, hawk-nosed or straight-nosed, thin-lipped or thick-lipped. All of them, in varying degrees, do have brown or reddish-brown skin, dark eyes, straight black hair, little beard and body hair, and broad cheekbones.

In 1500 A.D., there were about a million of these American Indians living in Alaska, Canada, and the United States. In addition, there were 90,000 or so Eskimos up in the Arctic. But the Eskimos weren't Indians. They looked more like the squat, flat-faced, narrow-eyed Chuckchis and other Mongoloid groups in northeastern Siberia than they did their Indian neighbors in Alaska and Canada, even though the latter were also Mongoloids.

Nor did these Indians all speak the same language. Eskimos did. An Alaskan Eskimo felt almost as comfortable talking to a Greenland Eskimo as a New Englander does in conversing with a native Californian. But that wasn't true with Indians. There were about as many different languages as there were tribes. And, according to anthropologists, there were some three hundred different Indian tribes in North America north of Mexico when Columbus crossed the Atlantic in 1492.

Many of these tribes, like the Havasupai and the Chiricahua Apaches, were small. Others, like the Cherokees and most of the Iroquoian tribes, numbered up into the thousands.

Nor were all Indians alike in their culture, their way of life. Some were hunters, some fishermen; others were seed gatherers, still others were farmers. Some lived in skin-covered tepees, some in bark wigwams; others lived in earth lodges or in stone apartment houses or in mud huts or brush shelters. Some Indians moved from camp to camp, following game animals or the ripening of wild fruits and seeds. Others lived in small villages; still others lived in big towns. Some Indians manufactured clay pots and pans, while a lot of other Indians didn't know how to make them. Some wove watertight baskets for cooking and storing food; others carved equally good storage containers out of wood; and still others made theirs out of birchbark. Some had well-stocked closets and cupboards; others barely managed to keep from starving. In short, no two Indian tribes lived exactly the same kind of life.

Yet anthropologists have also discovered that, in the same geographic region, most tribes had similar ways of life, one that differed from that of tribes in other geographic regions. The houses, implements, utensils, clothing, ceremonies and all the other things that make up a peoples' culture were more or less alike within any one geographic region.

Anthropologists call these geographic regions culture areas, identifying nine of them in the United States and Canada. These areas are listed below and are also shown on the accompanying map together with the names of the principal Indian tribes living in each one.

Northeastern Woodlands—This was a big culture area, extending from Hudson Bay in Canada southward along the Atlantic Coast to Virginia and westward through the Great Lakes and the Ohio River valley to and slightly beyond the Mississippi River. With the exception of the Iroquoian-speaking Indians of New York, most of the numerous Indian tribes in this area spoke Algonkian languages. The extreme northern Indians were mainly nomadic hunters and fishermen, while their southern relatives were farmers living in small to large villages. Although the Iroquois lived in large community houses called "longhouses," the Algonkians built smaller wigwams of birchbark.

Southeastern Woodlands—This area covered the southeastern United States, from the Ohio River to the Gulf of Mexico and from the Atlantic Ocean to and just beyond the Mississippi River. Less than half the size of its northern neighbor, this was one of the most densely populated regions in all of North America north of Mexico. Some 185,000 Indians called this home when the first Spanish explorers arrived in the sixteenth century. The largest and most important tribes were the Cherokees, Creeks, Choctaws, Chickasaws, Natchez, and Calusas. Practically all of them were farmers, living in grass or cane huts in large towns which were dominated by huge, flat-topped temple mounds.

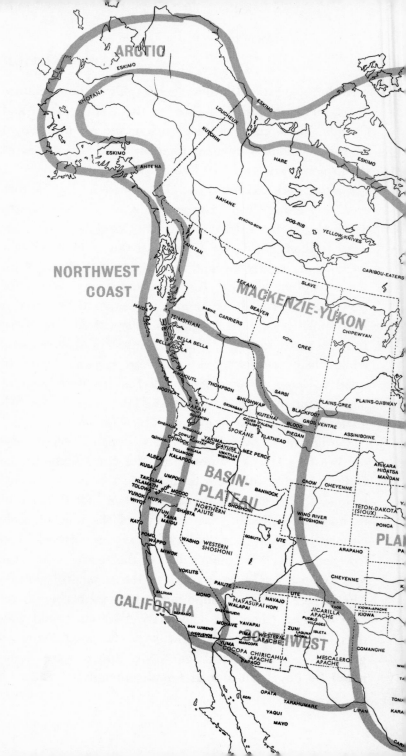

This map illustrates the approximate location of the nine cultural areas of the Indian tribes of North America

Kiowa Indian camp about 1870.

Plains—The Plains area was also big, running all the way from southern Canada to Texas and from the Mississippi River westward to the Rocky Mountains. This grassy plains country was the home of a great many different Indian tribes and the former home of millions of bison. Some of these Indians, like the Arikara, the Mandan, the Hidatsa, and the Omaha, were farmers and lived in earth-lodge villages along the Missouri River and its larger tributaries. Others, like the Blackfoot, the Cheyenne, the Comanche, the Kiowa, and the Dakota (Sioux), were nomadic hunters and gatherers and lived in portable, skin-covered tepees.

Southwest—This area includes the present-day states of Arizona, New Mexico, southwestern Colorado, southern Utah, southeastern Nevada, the western corner of Texas, and a slice of northern Mexico. The deserts and plateaus of the Southwest were the home of the prehistoric and historic Pueblo Indians and half a dozen different Apache tribes. It was also home to Pimas, Papagos, Yumas, Mohaves, Cocopas, Maricopas, Yavapais, Havasupais, and Walapais. With the exception of most of the Apaches, who were hunters and food gatherers, the rest of the Southwestern Indians were farmers. The Hopis and Zunis and other Pueblo Indians lived in stone and adobe apartment houses. The Indians in southern and western Arizona lived in circular, dome-shaped houses of poles and brush covered with earth.

A prehistoric Pueblo Indian cliff dwelling in Betakin, northern Arizona.

Taos Pueblo in New Mexico 1879.

The Navahos lived in earth-covered hogans, while the other Apaches lived in pole and brush wickiups.

Basin-Plateau—One of the driest sections of all, this area lies between the Rocky Mountains and the Sierra Nevada and Cascade Mountains of California, Oregon, and Washington, extending from British Columbia in Canada southward to Nevada and Utah. It was not over-populated, holding only some 64,000 Indians in the early

eighteenth century. The best known tribes were the
Nez Percé, the Flatheads, the Shoshonis, and the Utes
and Paiutes. Lacking agriculture, they were hunters,
fishers, and gatherers. Some of them often had to dig
up roots to keep from starving. In the south, their
homes were usually simple pole-and-brush shelters,
while the more northern Indians built large community
houses of arching poles covered with mats of tule or
cattail.

California—California rates a culture area all by itself. Five hundred years ago this was an Indian para-
dise, with some 85,000 Indians living there. There were
several hundred small tribes speaking a lot of different
languages. Typical tribes were the Maidu, Hupa, Chu-
mash, Modoc, Miwok, Pomo, and Karok. Living condi-
tions were excellent. The climate was mild enough that
most Indians could get by with a domed house built of
tule or grass thatch laid over a framework of poles. None
of these Indians were farmers. But there was an abundance of acorns and other wild plant foods and an even
greater abundance of fish in the rivers and ocean.

Northwest Coast—This area extended all along the
Pacific Coast from southeastern Alaska to southern Oregon. This was the former home of the totem pole and
the wealthiest Indians north of Mexico. Over 100,000
Indians were crowded into this narrow coastal belt.
The half-dozen distinct tribal groups included the
Tlingit, Haida, Kwakiutl, Tsimshian, Nootka, and Bellacoola. Food was even more abundant here than in California. The ocean teemed with salmon, sea otters, seals,
porpoises, and shellfish, while the forests abounded in

wild roots, bulbs, berries, deer, elk, and mountain goats. With an almost endless supply of giant cedar trees in their back yards, these Indians became excellent wood-carvers, building huge gable-roofed plank houses and decorating them with totem poles and other carvings.

Mackenzie-Yukon—This area covered interior Alaska and most of interior Canada, stretching from the Hudson Bay to the Yukon Valley in Alaska. It was the most thinly populated region in North America, inhabited by not many more than 30,000 hardy nomads. Practically all of them were Athabaskan-speaking Indians—the Hare, Yellowknife, Beaver, Slave, Kutchin, Sekani, Carrier, and several dozen other Indian tribes. They were hunters and fishermen, traveling by bark-covered canoes in the summer and snowshoes and toboggans in the winter. Few of them had permanent villages, generally getting along with temporary brush and bark shelters in the summer and tepee-like lodges or pole or log houses banked with moss or dirt in the winter.

Arctic—The Arctic culture area consisted of the 6,000 miles of coast fringing the continent from Alaska to Greenland and was the home of the Eskimo. Anthropologists estimate that there were about 90,000 Eskimos living there at the time of their discovery. From Alaska to Greenland, the various Eskimo tribes were remarkably alike in their looks, language, and way of life. All of them were hunters and fishermen, hunting caribou with bows and arrows and seals, walruses, and whales with harpoons. They used skin-covered kayaks in summer and dog sleds in winter. Some Eskimos built snow houses or igloos, while others built their winter dwell-

Hopi Indian youngsters dressed in ceremonial costumes for the Butterfly Dance.

ings out of stone, driftwood, or whalebone, covering them over with banked-up earth or sod.

Games were often closely linked to the customs and culture areas of the various Indian tribes. For example, hunting and warfare were favored in many games of the Plains and Woodlands Indians, while weather and corn were often featured in games of the Southwest Indians and salmon and fishing predominated in the tribes of the Northwest Coast.

TOPS, DOLLS, AND WHISTLES

1

Toys tell the story of man. Nearly every discovery or invention is, sooner or later, reflected in toys and games. Every change in the world of fashion is faithfully portrayed in the dress of dolls.

A visitor to the Earth from the Moon or Mars wouldn't have to be told that we are living in the Atomic or Space Age. All he would need would be one glance at any department store toy counter full of models of atomic-powered submarines, guns, space capsules, and astronaut suits.

One anthropologist divides Indian toys into three classes: 1) toys for soothing or amusing infants, such as rattles or feathers and other objects hung on cradles; 2) toys that children make for themselves out of clay or bits of wood or bark or stone; and 3) toys, like dolls and miniature utensils, which adults give to children for education or for ceremonial purposes.

Compared with today's thousands of different kinds of toys, American Indian toys were few in number and simple in construction. Five hundred years ago kids couldn't get the newest novelty toy by sending off ten cents and two box tops from packages of breakfast cereal. Like primitive children in other parts of the world, Indian boys and girls had to make the most of whatever was close at hand.

Yet most of the toys that have been found are similar to some of our modern toys. There were dolls, tops, rattles, whistles, noisemakers, models of dishes and other household equipment, bows and arrows, darts, balls, and even an occasional mechanical toy.

A rattle or jingle of some kind may have been the first toy some Indian boys or girls played with. At least one or more of these tinklers was probably the first thing a

SMITHSONIAN OFFICE OF ANTHROPOLOGY,
BUREAU OF AMERICAN ETHNOLOGY COLLECTION

Pima Indian gourd rattle.

baby saw dangling from the canopy of his cradle. Strings of animal claws or tiny birchbark cones or small white shells were often hung on a Chippewa baby's cradle. Sometimes Chippewa mothers would fill one of the birchbark cones with maple sugar so that the child could put it in his mouth and suck out some of the sweet sugar.

Labrador Eskimo children made toy rattles out of small skin drums enclosing a handful of pebbles, while Pueblo Indian children used natural rattles furnished by the dried seed pods of the rattlesnake plant. Some Indians also made natural rattles from wild gourds, with the seeds dried inside to make a noise.

But this wasn't the usual practice. To most Indians rattles were sacred objects, to be used only for rituals or dances or other ceremonial occasions. The rattle, for example, in Plains Indian sign language, is basic to all signs signifying that which is sacred.

Today, dolls are probably the most popular of all toys, and they seem to have been equally popular in all American Indian tribes. But there were no dolls that walked or talked or cried or drank from nursing bottles.

Indian dolls were probably idols or fetishes long before they became children's toys. Among a great many primitive, hunting- and gathering-tribes, including many others not so primitive, human figures or figurines were thought to possess some magical or supernatural power. They could, therefore, only be safely handled by a medicine man or some other individual trained in such ritualistic affairs. For this reason human figures in the form of dolls were taboo to the children of these tribes.

Most of the clay and stone figurines that archaeolo-

*Buckskin doll made by
the northern Plains In-
dians.*

gists have dug up in ancient ruins seem to have been images with magical or ceremonial significance.

Still other tribes, like the Chiricahua Apaches, didn't want their dolls to look too human because they were too much like the dead. For years Chiricahua mothers would not let their children have modern dolls, saying that they were "too natural."

Dolls were not just for girls. Small boys have always been interested in them. As a boy got older, however, he became more interested in carved animals and other more manly toys.

As you might expect, most dolls are female dolls. Even today, nine out of ten dolls are girl dolls. Nearly all of the prehistoric Basketmaker and Pueblo clay figures that archaeologists have found in Southwestern caves and cliff dwellings were feminine. So were the thousands of still older ones found in Mexico.

Dolls were made from wood, clay, stone, bone, ivory, animal skin, bark, corncobs, cornhusks, grass, or other plant fibers. Fathers, uncles or grandfathers usually carved well-shaped dolls for their children, nieces, or grandchildren. On the Northwest Coast, Nootka Indian women made dolls of shredded cedar bark for their little girls. Cheyenne and other Plains Indian women made dolls of deerskin for their daughters and nieces. Sometimes they also made tiny baby cradles which the girls could carry on their backs, in the same fashion in which the women carried their babies.

But some youngsters, particularly the older ones, made their own dolls. Indian children in the Eastern Woodlands frequently made their dolls out of corncobs

Chippewa Indian dolls made of cattails.

Chippewa Indian dolls made of pine needles.

and cornhusks. The husks were folded over the cob and tied across the top to mark the head, the tassel-like cornsilk became the doll's hair. Sometimes, to make the dolls more lifelike, the youngsters painted on the eyes, nose, and mouth. Fox Indian girls made clothing for their cornhusk dolls out of muskrat and squirrel skins.

Arapaho girls often made simple armless and legless dolls out of a piece of buckskin and buffalo hair or grass. A small ball of grass or buffalo hair was placed in the center of the buckskin and tied about with sinew cord to hold it in place. The ball represented the doll's head, the tied place the neck, and the hanging folds of buckskin the body. A second strip of buckskin might be wrapped about the doll in imitation of the robes or blankets worn by the grownups.

Indian girls played with their dolls just like twentieth-century girls do. They sang lullabies to them, dressed and undressed them, and, as they got older, made aprons, moccasins, robes, and other articles of feminine clothing.

Pima, Papago, and Pueblo Indian youngsters in Arizona and New Mexico were fortunate enough to have scraps of native cotton cloth to use as clothing for their dolls.

And so did many Mexican and Central American Indian girls. But the rest of the Indian children in North America had to be satisfied with buckskin or other animal skin, strips of woven grass or bark mats.

Hopi Indian children in northern Arizona also had another kind of doll—the kachina doll. Kachinas, to the Hopis, were supernatural beings who lived on high

These Hopi kachina dolls are representations of masked super-natural beings.

mountains, like the San Francisco Peaks near Flagstaff. During certain Hopi ceremonies, kachinas were impersonated by men wearing elaborate masks. Using dried cottonwood roots, Hopi men carved and painted small figurines to represent the different masked dancers. There were over two hundred and fifty different kinds of kachinas, each with its own set of distinguishing features. Like Santa Claus bringing gifts, the kachina dancers gave to the youngsters the different kachina dolls made especially for them by their relatives.

But these kachina dolls were not real dolls. They were taken home and hung up on the wall or from a roof beam. There they sat, not as toys or dolls but as object lessons to educate the children about the religious meaning of kachinas and to teach them the differences between kachinas.

The doll was also a favorite toy of Eskimo children. Eskimo dolls were generally carved from wood, ivory, or bone and ranged from an inch to a foot or more in length. Some of these dolls even had moveable parts. One doll carved out of bone had its head fitted on a wooden peg projecting from the neck so that the head could be turned like a swivel. Another similarly made wooden doll had an ingenious system of cords so that the head could be turned to the right or to the left. Some of these Eskimo dolls were also adorned with bracelets, bead necklaces, nose rings and earrings. Sometimes the legs of dolls were made of skin, stuffed with hair or grass, to make them look more realistic. To go with their dolls, Eskimo girls usually had complete outfits of toy boots, mittens, and skin clothing

patterned after the clothing used by themselves and their parents. They also had toy models of houses, bedding, and grass mats.

The ball has furnished amusement for both youngsters and grownups for thousands of years. Not only is the ball old but it is probably used in more kinds of games than any other toy. A ball can be thrown or caught, rolled or bounced, kicked or batted.

Balls can be made of almost anything. Even solid stone balls have been dug up in ancient ruins. Nor does a ball necessarily have to be round. The bladder from almost any animal, after it has been cleaned and blown up with air and tied, makes a perfectly good ball that will even bounce. Nearly every Indian tribe knew how to make this kind of ball. And the Indians also made balls out of deerskin or other animal skin filled with cornhusks, cedar bark, moss, grass, feathers, deer or buffalo hair, or human hair. And frequently they carved balls out of wood or stone.

Some American Indian youngsters even played with rubber balls. This was something Old World children couldn't do until after the sixteenth-century Spanish explorers brought back rubber balls from Mexico to Europe. The Indians in Mexico and Central America and northern South America were the first to discover that the milky sap of certain tropical plants could be made into rubber and that this in turn could be made into elastic balls. In fact, along the east coast of Mexico lived one Indian tribe, the Olmecs, whose name means Rubber People. Mayas, Aztecs, Totonacs, Olmecs, Zapotecs, and other Mexican and Central American In-

ARIZONA STATE MUSEUM
Alaskan Eskimo doll.

dian tribes all played with these rubber balls. So did some of the Indians who used to live in southern and central Arizona. But that's about as far north as rubber balls strayed. And, as we shall see later, most of these rubber balls were used in ceremonial games played by adults.

Tops were also widely used by American Indian youngsters. Spin-the-top was the first game played by Hidatsa Indian boys, as it was in many other Indian tribes. According to most anthropologists, tops probably originated in ancient China or Japan many thousands of years ago. At least, throughout the Orient, there are hundreds of different kinds of tops, more than are to be found any place else in the world. To name only a few, there are whipping tops, pinching tops, catching tops, fighting tops, whistling tops, tops lit up with tiny lanterns, shell tops weighted with lead, humming tops, and many, many others. From Asia, tops found their way, either by trade or by migrations of peoples, across the Bering Strait to the New World. But only the simplest kinds of tops ever reached North America.

As you might expect, the people living closest to the Bering Strait, the Eskimos, were champion top-spinners. Both Eskimo boys and girls liked to spin tops. But these tops were not the same as the tops we play with today— the cone-shaped wooden tops, pointed at one end, that you spin with a tightly wound string or the plastic or metal musical tops that you wind with a key to make them whirl around and play a tune at the same time.

Eskimo tops were usually disk-shaped pieces of ivory or wood or bone, from 2 to 5 inches in diameter, with a hole in the center through which a round wooden or

Eskimo ivory, wooden, and bone tops from Alaska.

bone peg protruded above and below. The bottom part of the peg furnished the point on which the top could spin while the upper part was twirled between the hands to set the top to spinning.

In winter, when the ground was frozen and the days were too short to play outside for any length of time, Eskimo boys and girls in Alaska played a top-spinning game. One youngster would set his top to spinning on the floor of the house. Then he would run out through the entrance and try to make a complete circle around the house and back in again before his top stopped spinning. Then one after the other, the rest would try their luck.

The favorite kind of top for most American Indian boys was the whip top. This was generally a cylindrical piece of wood, roughly peg-shaped and pointed at one end. The top was spun between the fingers to get it

Dakota Indian whip tops and whip.

started and then was kept in motion by striking it with a whip. These whips usually had from two to four, 18- to 24-inch strands of buckskin tied to the end of a wooden handle a foot or two long. An expert could keep one of these whip tops spinning almost indefinitely and could actually make it hum.

To spin a top, a flat or level surface is needed. And it should also be fairly hard. Up in the Arctic and in the cold northern Plains, Eskimo and Cheyenne and Arapaho boys spun their tops in winter on the ice or on frozen ground. But Hopi and other Indian boys living in the warmer southland where there wasn't much ice had to use the hard-packed clay floor of the village plaza or any other level piece of hard ground.

Hopi Indian youngsters, both boys and girls, spun wooden tops whittled for them by their fathers or older brothers. The boys' tops were usually painted with white,

ARIZONA STATE MUSEUM

Hopi Indian wooden tops and rawhide whips.

red, or black bands, while the girls tops were plain. Children sometimes ran races by whipping their tops ahead of them. Older boys occasionally played a team top-game. Each player tried to whip his top so that it would jump and touch an opponent's top, putting that player out of the game. Hopi youngsters could only play with tops in the early spring. Their humming noise, which sounded like the wind, was thought to bring wind. Wind storms in early spring were all right. But at any other time of the year they would be too destructive to young plants.

Blackfoot Indian boys spun birchwood tops on ice or hard-packed snow. Tops were started with a quick twist of the wrist and kept spinning with strokes from the deerskin lashes of a willow-handled whip. One of their favorite top games was to see who could spin his top the greatest distance around a 20-foot circle of hard-trampled snow. Small cross trenches were dug at intervals to furnish extra hazards. It required considerable skill to whip a top so that it would jump a trench and still keep spinning around the circle after it landed. The winner kept the loser's top. Another Blackfoot top game was played on river ice, with round stones taking the place of the wooden tops. Two boys would spin their stone tops and whip them together as hard as they could. Whichever boy's stone top cracked the other's or continued to spin the longest after the collision was the winner.

Arapaho boys also made their hardwood tops fight, whipping them so that one would hit the other. The boy whose top split first was the loser.

Chippewa boys, like Blackfoot boys, spun smoothstone tops on ice, setting the stone in motion with the fingers and keeping it spinning by striking it with a rawhide whip tied to a wooden handle.

Although most tops were made of wood, Nootka Indian boys made theirs out of bone or ivory. Some Cheyenne and Arapaho tops were carved out of bone, while some Dakota and Hidatsa tops were made of horn. Among some of the pottery-making tribes, tops were even molded of clay and baked hard so they wouldn't break easily. In Arizona, Maricopa Indian youngsters stuck 6-inch long sticks of wood through disks of clay and twirled them between their palms to make the toys spin like tops.

Like boys and girls today, Indian children loved anything that would make a racket, the louder the racket the better. One of the noisiest was the bull-roarer, also known as the buzzer or whizzer or whizzing stick. This curious instrument was a thin, flat, rectangular slat of wood from 6 inches to 2 feet in length, with a long cord tied to one end. When the piece of wood was whirled rapidly around the head at the end of the cord, it gave a distinctive roaring or whizzing sound.

To most Indian tribes, the bull-roarer was a sacred implement, closely allied to lightning and thunder and rain. The Hopi Indians thought its whizzing sound represented the wind that accompanied thunderstorms, while

Dakota Indian bull-roarer.

the Navaho Indians thought it represented the voice of
the thunderbird, the giant bird which was believed to
make thunder by flapping its wings and to make lightning by opening and closing its eyes. In fact, many
Apache, Hopi, and Zuni bull-roarers have lightning symbols carved or painted on them.

The bull-roarer might have been a sacred implement
to a lot of Indian tribes. But it made a fine racket and
many Eskimo and Indian children were quick to adopt
it as a toy. Eskimo boys, not having an abundance of
wood, often carved bull-roarers out of thin blades of bone
or ivory. Dakota and other Indians tied a stick to the
end of the cord to serve as a handle. Maricopa Indians
made a play bull-roarer out of a 10-inch length of split
and scraped arrowweed, with a cord tied in notches
across one end.

Some tribes, however, put definite restrictions on the
use of bull-roarers. Hopi youngsters, for example, couldn't
whirl them just any old time they felt like it. Like tops,
they were allowed to use them only in the early spring,
when the wind which the bull-roarer invariably brought
wouldn't damage anything. Nor did the Chiricahua
Apache elders like to see their youngsters play with bull-
roarers or other similar noisemakers. Whenever the
elders caught children playing with bull-roarers, they
scolded them, saying it would bring wind. Paiute elders
had the same belief. In fact, Paiute children weren't
allowed to whip the air with switches as this, too, would
call the wind.

A somewhat similar noisemaking toy common among
Eskimo children as well as among Plains and Southwest

Indian youngsters was the buzz or whirligig. This was a whirling toy made of a flat piece of pottery, bone, stone, or gourd shell, or of a heavy bone, with one or more cords on either side. Twisting and pulling on these cords caused the disk to spin around and around. Some Eskimo buzzers had a couple of holes drilled through them so they could be strung on an endless sinew cord. By alternately tightening and relaxing the string, one could make the disk twirl around with a humming sound. Chiricahua Apache youngsters made an almost identical buzz by cutting two holes in a piece of hide.

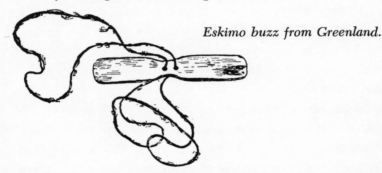

Eskimo buzz from Greenland.

That this was an extremely old toy is evident since stone disks with two perforations have been found in prehistoric Southwestern cliff dwellings.

Another noisemaker that found its way into the world of Indian toys was the whistle. Archaeologists have dug up hundreds of bone whistles in prehistoric ruins all over North America. These whistles were simply short tubes of bird or animal bone with circular holes drilled through one side. Similar whistles made of pottery have also been found. Like the bull-roarer, many of these whistles may have been used primarily in ceremonies and ceremonial

Prehistoric Pueblo Indian bone whistles.

performances. Nootka Indian youngsters, for example, were not allowed to play with whistles since they were used in many of their rituals. But anthropologists have seen children using them when they were playing well away from the village where adults couldn't see or hear them.

Paiute Indian children in northern California and Nevada made whistles out of the stems of the horsetail plant, while other Indians made them out of pieces of wood.

Still another noisemaker was the popgun, although there is some question as to its existence among the Indians before white contact in the sixteenth and seventeenth centuries. However, a couple of well-made wooden popguns dug up in a prehistoric ruin in Peru point to the probability that this was a true native toy long before the time of Christopher Columbus. Popguns have been found among the Arikara and Cheyenne and some of the Siouan tribes in the Plains, among the Sauk and Fox Indians in Iowa, among the Yokuts Indians in California, and among the Jicarilla Apaches in New Mexico. All of these toy popguns were much alike, consisting of a foot-long tube of wood fitted with a piston for shooting wads of bark or other fibers or small stones.

One of the noisiest of all toy noisemakers that still shatter the peace and quiet of many homes today is the

Wooden popgun used by the Sauk and Fox Indians.

drum. Drums were also common in nearly every American Indian tribe. But most of them didn't look like the drums you see today. Double-headed hide drums, similar to modern drums, were not used in all tribes. And where they have been found, they may be of comparatively modern introduction.

The Eskimo and some of the more northern Indian tribes had tambourine-like drums—a single skin stretched over a hoop to form a single-headed drum—which were probably derived from Asia by way of the Bering Strait. Mexican and Central American Indians had hollow, so-called log drums. The pottery kettle-drum, a skin stretched tight over the mouth of a clay pot, probably originated in this southern area and spread northward into the Southwest and the Southeast and up into the Plains. Frequently, kettle drums were partially filled with water to give them a better tone. Foot drums, consisting of a plank over a pit, were also used on the Northwest Coast, California, and adjacent areas.

Practically all of these drums seem to have been either war drums or sacred drums or ceremonial drums used in ritual dances. Among the Eskimo, for example, the tambourine was the badge of the medicine man. Probably few of these or of the other kinds of drums ever became toys for youngsters to bang on just to make a racket.

Can we call a knife a toy? Probably—and particularly if it happens to be a boy's first knife. With it, he can cut and carve and whittle his own whistles and popguns and anything else he wants to make. And it was easy for an American Indian boy to get his hands on a knife. There were always plenty of sharp pieces of flint lying

about the camp or village. Some were broken and dis-
carded knife blades or spear points, while others may
have been imperfect knives thrown away during manu-
facture. But any one of them was big enough and sharp
enough for a boy anxious to cut off a willow sapling for a
whistle.

Some Alaskan Eskimo children had their own special
knives—snow knives. These were from 4 to 15 inches long,
made of bone or ivory, with a curved blade and a handle
frequently carved to represent the head of a salmon or a
seal or a sea gull. Both boys and girls used these snow
knives as toys, carving the hard-packed snow into fan-
tastic figures of birds and seals and bears. Then they
would run at the figures and cut them to pieces with their
snow knives, in imitation of the killing of game by
hunters.

Many Indian children also had as toys small figures of
birds and animals carved for them by their fathers or
uncles out of wood, bone, or ivory. Or, as among the
Jicarilla Apaches, toy animals might be made from the
skins of chipmunks, squirrels, wood rats, or other small
animals, which were sewn together and then stuffed
with grass.

Eskimo youngsters had more than their share of toy
figures of birds, seals, bears, and other animals carved
from ivory or bone or deerhorn. As playthings, they had
toy ivory boats and toy sleds carved of ivory and pulled
by tiny ivory dogs attached to the sled with sinew cords.

Some of these Eskimo toy figures were even mechanical. For example, a wooden woodpecker was so mounted
on a board that by pulling on a string, which was fastened

to the bird's beak and passed down through a hole in the board, you would cause the woodpecker's head to bob up and down as if the bird were pecking at the red dots representing food that were painted on the board. Another similar toy was a mechanical mouse. A long flat board was drilled with half a dozen holes, all lined up in a row. Then a long cord was run in and out of these holes and the ends tied to a small strip of fur. Pulling on the cord made the fur dart in and out of the holes like a mouse.

Down in Mexico, archaeologists have unearthed a number of small pottery toys—clay dogs and jaguars and other figures—all equipped with clay disks that look like wheels. But the American Indians seem not to have understood the real meaning of the wheel and what could be done with it since wheels have not been found anywhere else except on these Mexican toys.

Archaeologists aren't certain that stilts were used as toys by Indian youngsters in prehistoric days. We do know that stilts made of wooden poles, with a forked notch for the foot, have been found among a number of tribes in Wyoming, Arizona, New Mexico, Oklahoma, and Mexico and on southward into South America. And some of the ancient Mayan hieroglyphics show figures that appear to be walking on stilts.

Still another toy that we don't know too much about is the sling. Aztecs and many South American Indians used slingshots as weapons. But the Indians of the United States and Canada never seem to have taken to the sling The few tribes that did pick it up used it as a toy, not a weapon. Klamath and Paiute boys, for example, played with deerhide slings, using small stones as ammunition.

RUN, CHIEF, RUN

2

In play, Indian children had the run of the camp or village. Parents couldn't tell their youngsters to stay in their own yards and play since few Indian houses had such a thing as a front or back yard. Nor were Indian youngsters continually being told not to touch this or that or not to do this or that. It didn't matter if they spilled something on the dirt floor of the house. It could be cleaned up in a jiffy. And there was little breakable furniture in most houses. The Hopi child, for example, was warned about getting too near the edge of the sheer cliffs surrounding the villages, and he was warned about going too close to a fire. But aside from these and a few other simple prohibitions, he, along with most other Indian youngsters, was free from most of the restrictions imposed upon the modern city child.

In this chapter we shall tell you something about the simpler Indian games, games requiring little or no equipment, games like tag and follow-the-leader and crack-the-whip and hide-and-seek and tug-of-war and running and relay races and high-jump and broad-jump contests and wrestling and such unusual games as the holding-one's-breath game and the laughing game.

Blind-man's-buff (hide-and-seek) and tag and follow-the-leader were especially popular with Indian youngsters, just as they still are in the twentieth century.

Follow-the-leader was played by boys and girls of numerous tribes throughout the United States and Canada. In many tribes the game was called Crooked Path or Twisted Trail, probably because the leader would try to set as winding and twisting a course as possible.

Tag was equally popular with most Indian youngsters, and there were many different kinds of tag games. On the Northwest Coast, Nootka children played a game that was a combination of tag and crack-the-whip. They joined hands in a circle and ran sideways until they were running as fast as they could. When they suddenly let go of hands, those who had become dizzy and were off balance fell down and were "it." These youngsters then chased the rest. Each one that was caught also became "it" and helped catch the others. The game ended when everyone had been caught.

Blackfoot Indian girls also played a combination game of tag and crack-the-whip. Seven or eight of them would form a line, each girl hanging on to the waist of the one in front. As they ran, the leader would try to swing the line so that she could turn and tag the girl at the end of the line. This latter girl had to keep her place in line, but she could duck and twist around to avoid being tagged. If the leader succeeded in tagging her, the girl that was tagged became the leader and the girl in front of her became the last in line.

Some Northwest Coast Indians played a tag game called Fish Trap. One player, known as the "fish," was given a short head start. Then the other ten or fifteen "fishermen" joined hands and tried to catch the "fish" in their net.

Hopi Indian girls played a tag game that was somewhat out of the ordinary. The leader laid out a complicated, twisting pathway in soft sand, ending up near the center of that particular play area. The players lined up at the beginning of the path and ran along it toward the center, with the leader chasing them. If a girl slipped off the path, she was out of the game. The first girl that the leader caught became "it" and had to chase the others on the next trip.

Fox Indian youngsters played tag much like we play the game today. The children would draw straws from a bundle to see which one would be "it." To be caught, a youngster had to be tapped squarely on the head.

Nootka children also played another game somewhat like tag. One youngster would throw a clam shell as far as he could down the beach. All the other youngsters would then run after it and try to be the first to pick it up. The one who recovered it got chased until he threw it as far as he could and the game would begin all over again.

Nootka boys and girls also used a clam shell for a rough-and-tumble team game. One team would bury a clam shell in a pile of sand. Then one of the team members would sit on top of the sand pile to guard the shell, not unlike a "King of the Castle." While his teammates defended him, the opposing team would try to drag him off and uncover the shell. If they succeeded in getting it, it was their turn to bury the shell in the sand pile.

Hide-and-seek or blind-man's-buff was also a popular game with most Indian youngsters. Chippewa Indian children played two different types of hide-and-seek. In one, called the Butterfly game, the hunter was chosen by the drawing of lots. He had to cover his eyes while the other children hid. When he began his search, he sang "Butterfly, show me where to go." In the second version the child was blindfolded and tried to catch the other youngsters as they ran away.

Nootka children played a team hide-and-seek game. One team hid and the other team hunted for them. If anyone happened to hide so well he or she couldn't be found, the searchers called his name and shouted insults to try to make him answer and give away his hiding place.

In addition to the usual hide-and-seek game, Chiricahua Apache children played a game something like blind-man's-buff, with an arrow as the prize. One of the youngsters was blindfolded and an arrow was stuck in the ground some distance away. If the boy found the arrow, it was his to keep. Sometimes several arrows might be stuck in the ground. If the blindfolded boy was able to find one, then all the rest belonged to him.

Alaskan Eskimo youngsters also played blind-man's-buff. One of the players was blindfolded and the others stood in a broad circle around him. At a given signal all of them uttered one loud shout. After that they kept as quiet as possible, creeping about on the ground or hiding in the tall grass to avoid being caught. The first person to be captured was in turn blindfolded.

To Chippewa youngsters, their most exciting hide-and-seek game was the Windigo game. The windigo were believed to be a mysterious tribe of awesome beings who were cannibals. Any stranger coming into a village was carefully watched because he could be a windigo. Chippewa children turned this into a game. One youngster was chosen by lot to play the part of the windigo. Putting branches and leaves on his head to make himself look weird and grotesque, the windigo hid in a clump of bushes. The other youngsters then lined up one behind the other and went hunting for the windigo. When they came close to his hiding place, he rushed out at them, yelling and making hideous faces and pretending he wanted to eat them alive. The younger children clung close together, screaming, while the leader fought with the windigo. This was a favorite game with Chippewa youngsters.

Older Hopi boys played a hide-and-seek game at night. Called the Witch game, one of the players was chosen as the witch and given a small drum. After he had hidden himself, the other players tried to find him. If the boys strayed too far off in the wrong direction, the witch beat his drum and quickly sneaked away to another hiding place. When the witch was finally run down and caught, another boy was selected to act as the witch and the game started all over again.

Tug-of-war was also a popular game. Among the Alaskan Eskimo, the two leaders locked hands while the teams lined up behind them, each with his arms grasping the

Hopi Indian Pueblo of Oraibi in 1933.

person in front. Northwest Coast and Hopi and Chiricahua Apache youngsters were also fond of playing tug-of-war games.

Hopi Indians, both youngsters and adults, often reversed the usual procedure and played push-of-war, trying to shove their opponents backward. Nor was this always a game played just for fun. In 1906, two factions in the Hopi Pueblo of Oraibi agreed to settle a dispute by a push-of-war in which the losers had to move out and build a town of their own. In the ensuing game, the liberals pushed the conservatives back across a line drawn on the ground, and the latter group immediately packed up and founded the village of Hotevilla a few miles away.

Along the Northwest Coast laughing games were popular and were played by both adults and children. Laughing games were often played by two individuals, such as a husband and wife. Youngsters usually formed two teams. Sometimes they lined up in two rows and stood staring at each other, their faces showing as little expression as possible. The first side to break down and smile or laugh lost the game. Or each side might choose a champion. While these two faced each other, the members of the two teams did everything they could—from making faces to shouting humorous remarks—to try to make the champion of the other side laugh. When one of the two finally changed expression or smiled or laughed, he was replaced by a teammate. According to the older Indians, Northwest Coast youngsters used to play several other variations of this laughing game.

In one of these variations, played by the Chinook Indians along the Columbia River, the boys stood behind one pile of sand while the girls were behind another pile of sand a hundred feet away. Each side set up a stick as a marker in its sand pile and dared the other side to come and get it. When one side took up the challenge, the members of the other side began laughing and calling, trying to make the approaching group laugh. If they were successful in this, the losers had to go back behind their sand pile and the winners then tried to get the other side's marker without laughing.

Another unusual game of the Northwest Coast Nootka Indians was a test of lung capacity. A group of youngsters picked the longest fern stem they could find and broke off the alternate branches. Then each youngster in turn took the fern and touched one branch after the other, each time saying "pina" without taking a breath. The one who managed to go farthest down the stalk before running out of breath was the winner of the game.

Klamath Indian children in southern Oregon also had a breath-holding game. A group would run forward, cry-

ing "wo yi" as long as their breath held out and stopping
at the spot where they ran out of breath. The one who
went the farthest won the game.

An ancient Eskimo game, one which still ranks as a
national sport in our forty-ninth state, was skin tossing
or blanket tossing. A large walrus hide was stretched out
flat and while one of the players stood in the center of
the skin, the others jerked the skin upward, throwing the
person on it high in the air. If he landed on his feet, some-
one on the other side had to take his place. If he didn't,
he or one of his teammates had to remain on the skin. A
player might be tossed as high as 15 or 20 feet into the
air at each bounce.

Blackfoot Indian boys also had a blanket-tossing team
game. Boys on one side would toss a small boy from the
other side in a buffalo robe or blanket. If they could toss
the boy so high that he would cry out that he had had
enough, they won. If they couldn't, the other side won.

A number of tribes, such as the Crow in Montana,
had tongue-twisters like our "Peter Piper picked a peck
of pickled peppers," which had to be uttered at break-
neck speed without error.

Indian children of most tribes also imitated their elders
in athletic contests. They had all kinds of foot races,
relay races, obstacle races, and broad-jump and high-
jump contests. Even girls occasionally ran races. Arapaho Indian boys ran races nearly every evening as a part
of their physical training as future warriors. Hidatsa
youngsters in North Dakota also ran foot races in imitation of young men getting ready for war.

Wrestling matches were common in many North American Indian tribes. Eskimos, particularly, were fond of wrestling contests, as were both Blackfoot and Chiricahua Apache Indians.

Where there was plenty of water, in rivers or lakes or the ocean, Indian youngsters took up swimming at an early age. Along the lower Colorado River the Yuma Indians loved the water and swam at all seasons of the year. Arapaho and other Plains Indian children practically lived in or next to the water during the warmer months of the year. So did Northwest Coast youngsters, who played in the ocean where it was warmed by the Japanese current. But up in Alaska and northern Canada and Greenland the waters were much colder, and few Eskimo children ever learned how to swim.

The north country, however, had its compensations. The coming of winter might signal the end of most fair-weather sports and games; but it brought with it lots of snow and ice. And Eskimo and Indian children had just as much fun on the snowy hills and ice-covered rivers and lakes near their winter villages. They acted like today's youngsters—making snowballs and throwing them at targets or at each other, sliding down hills on pieces of bark or skin or other makeshift sleds.

Some ingenious Plains Indian boys made sleds out of five to ten buffalo rib-bones with willow crossbars tied tightly together with rawhide. As boys often do today, they tried to see who could coast the greatest distance down a hill and out across the valley.

Blackfoot and Cheyenne and other Plains Indian youngsters also coasted down snow-covered hills on buffalo hides. Their mothers kept a sharp eye on these sliders. But they weren't watching the youngsters as

much as they were keeping track of the wear and tear
on the buffalo-hide sleds. This was a labor-saving method
of softening the hides and rubbing off the hair. Once the
hair was worn off, the mothers took the hides to cut them
up for moccasin soles and rawhide cord.

Blackfoot boys and girls made a game out of seeing
who could hop the farthest on one leg in deep snow. Both
Hopi boys and girls engaged in snow battles.

In northeastern North America most Indians used
toboggans to get around in winter. Probably Indian children living in this area had their parents make smaller
versions so that they could slide down snow-covered
slopes. Up in the Arctic, Eskimo youngsters frequently
harnessed puppies to toy sleds.

Puppies and other pets, probably shouldn't be classi-
fied as either toys or games. Yet the Eskimos and Indians
did use them in many of their games. Plains Indian
girls frequently pretended that small puppies were their
babies, dressing them up like dolls and strapping them
into their baby cradles and carrying them on their
backs.

Dogs were the most common pets since, except for bees
and a few turkeys, the dog was the North American Indian's only domesticated animal. Boys and girls also
caught young birds, rabbits, prairie dogs, and other small
animals and kept them as pets. Blackfoot boys captured
baby hawks in their nests and put them in woven willow
cages, keeping them until the birds had grown feathers
long enough for use on arrows. Nootka youngsters captured hummingbirds by smearing slug slime on twigs. The
birds were then tied to a string so the children could
play with them by making them fly around and around.

MUD BALLS AND MUD PIES

3

Ponca Indian boys along the Missouri River played a game which they called "Mud-on-a-stick." This game was a form of mock warfare. The two groups opposing each other pretended to be warriors from two different tribes. Each player would arm himself with a willow branch and mold a ball of sticky mud on the end of it. The two sides would then fight by throwing the mud balls at each other from the end of their willow sticks. The battle came to an end only when the young warriors of both sides were plastered with mud from head to foot.

The nearby river then came in handy to wash off all traces of the fighting before the boys showed up at home.

Blackfoot Indian boys played what they called the "clay war-game." Each boy cut a willow stick 5 or 6 feet long and made himself a supply of ammunition by rolling wet clay into balls about 2 inches in diameter. Then two opposing groups faced each other about 50 yards apart and began firing. Older Blackfoot men who had played the game in their youth claimed that the long whippy sticks threw the clay pellets with such force that they flew through the air like bullets.

Fox Indian boys fought similar sham battles with soft mud or clay thrown from the end of a stick.

Chiricahua Apache boys, living in southeastern Arizona and southwestern New Mexico in a land of few rivers, didn't waste what little mud they had in mock warfare. Instead, they stuck small pellets of mud on the end of a willow stick and whipped them at birds.

But other southern Arizona Indians were lucky enough to have plenty of mud for mimic warfare. The Gila River flowed through the front or back yards of most Maricopa Indian boys, furnishing them with an abundant supply of mud. For mud fights, two lines of boys would oppose each other, each boy armed with a big chunk of mud under one arm and a stick a foot or 2 long. Pinching off a small lump of mud, each boy would put it on the end of the stick so that it could be thrown at the other side. The war began at a prearranged signal. The boys could dodge, but they had to keep their line intact. If they were hit, they were not supposed to cry out or run away. This was their first training as future warriors, teaching them to throw straight and to hold their place in battle. The two lines moved toward each other, slinging mud, until one side finally broke and ran. Then both the winners and losers adjourned to the river to wash off the mud.

Ponca boys found another use for mud. They would hollow out a clay ball or boat by rolling sticky clay or mud on their elbows. Then they would set this floating on the water, and putting balls of mud on the end of sticks, throw the mud balls at the floating clay boat. When a mud ball hit the target, the boat would explode with a loud pop.

Indian youngsters also used mud or clay for making miniature pots and pans and bowls that looked just like the bigger ones their mothers made for cooking and carrying water and storing corn and beans and seeds.

At prehistoric Pueblo Bonito (Spanish for "beautiful village") in Chaco Canyon, New Mexico, now a national monument, Indian children were playing with miniature bowls and ladles and pitchers as far back as the eleventh century. Some of these pots were crude and were probably made by the youngsters themselves. But others that were well-shaped and even decorated with black designs painted on a white background were undoubtedly fashioned by Indian mothers and given to their little girls as toys. Large fragments of broken bowls and jars with the edges smoothed off seem to indicate that the children raided the village rubbish heap for odds and ends that could be turned into dishes or other useful toys.

In prehistoric Indian villages in Georgia and Virginia

Small clay jars, bowls, and ladles made by prehistoric Pueblo Indians in Arizona and New Mexico.

and Missouri and Kansas and in a dozen or two other states, archaeologists have dug up more of these miniature clay dippers and bowls and jars. Judging from the numbers of these toy pots and pans that have been found, the Indian children in these areas must have played house a lot.

Even today, Hopi Indian girls play at making pottery, shaping small pots out of clay. Sometimes they sun-dry them and sometimes they actually fire them just like their mothers do. Pima Indian girls used to mold mud dishes on their elbows. After a few minutes drying in the hot desert sun, the dishes were ready for use.

The prehistoric Pueblo Indian cliff dwelling of Keet Seel in northern Arizona.

Along the Gila River in southern Arizona, five-year old Maricopa Indian girls imitated their mothers in making pots and pans. Working up a ball of mud, they beat it out flat and pinched up the sides to form a miniature vessel which was then set in the sun to dry.

Indian youngsters in tribes where pottery making was unknown in prehistoric times probably still managed to make mud pies. And many of them undoubtedly made dishes out of mud or clay in imitation of the bowl-shaped baskets manufactured by their mothers. And most of these youngsters also probably played with miniature baskets made for them by their mothers or older sisters. A number of Indian tribes, particularly the Pomo and other California and Pacific Coast tribes, used baskets for everything from baby cradles and fish traps to cooking pots and water jars. Being master artisans, it was nothing for these basket makers to make tiny baskets as toys for their children. In some tribes, girls of seven or eight were taught how to weave baskets and, as a result, made their own play baskets.

Not all miniature baskets were used as toys. Many of the tiny Pomo baskets you see in museums today, some so small that a half dozen of them can be hidden in a thimble, were originally woven for trade with the early

ARIZONA STATE MUSEUM

Miniature baskets made by the Pomo Indians of California, with two small Pima Indian baskets on the left.

Papago Indian girls weaving baskets.

white settlers. Papago Indians in southern Arizona weave miniature baskets for still another reason. Papagos traditionally leave a miniature basket or some other similar token in exchange for sahuaro cactus fruit or other things which they take from nature.

In addition to tiny mud pots and pans and baskets, most Indian children also had other miniature household equipment—tepees or wigwams or brush huts, baby cradles, mats of plaited rushes or reeds, hide robes or blankets, and digging sticks and other implements and utensils. With these and their dolls and toy bows and arrows, both girls and boys played house, trying to imitate the home life of their parents.

Hopi youngsters, using wet mud, built models of the

stone pueblos in which they lived. Around them they fashioned make-believe fields and gardens by sticking twigs and leaves into the ground. On toy grinding stones the girls pretended to grind corn into meal, while the boys took their small bows and arrows and went out hunting. Sometimes the girls didn't have to pretend that dolls were their babies since they had to look after their one- or two-year old baby brother or sister.

Some Indian children, like the Chiricahua Apaches, made brush huts big enough to play inside. In them, they entertained their playmates and served them food concocted of mud and sticks.

Many Indian children also played with small clay figures of birds and animals which they themselves made. In the prehistoric pueblo of Kinishba, in eastern Arizona, archaeologists uncovered crudely shaped figures of turkey, deer, bear, foxes, and mountain sheep. All were quite small, from 1 to 3 inches long and from 1 to 2 inches high. Navaho children still build little play houses and corrals and stock them with tiny molded clay figurines of horses and sheep and other animals.

ARIZONA STATE MUSEUM

Miniature clay animals made by the prehistoric Pueblo Indians of Arizona.

BUTTON, BUTTON

Games of pure ingenuity and calculation, such as our chess and checkers, were entirely unknown in prehistoric North America. Nor did the Indians have playing cards until these were brought in by European explorers and settlers in the sixteenth and seventeenth centuries.

But the Indians never missed them. Their place was more than filled by guessing games or games of chance. To the North American Indians, these games were the most popular of all their amusements. Few public gatherings or ceremonies were complete without their games of chance. And nearly all of these games, including most sporting contests and ball games, were invariably accompanied by betting.

More often than not the stakes in these games were high. A man might risk all of his property, including his loin cloth and blanket, on a single game. Players were known to gamble away their wives and even their own scalps.

Although these guessing games and other gambling games were primarily adult games, for men or women only, the youngsters of most tribes played modified versions of practically all of them. Younger children usually played just for the fun of playing. But the older ones frequently imitated their elders and wagered arrows or other similar items on the outcome of the game.

One of the most common of the guessing games was the hidden-ball game, an aboriginal variation of our familiar game of "Button, button, who's got the button?"

Also called the moccasin game, the hidden-ball game was a game in which a small object was hidden in one of several places (usually four). The opponents then tried to guess where the object was concealed. The hidden object might be a small piece of wood or horn, a rounded chunk of animal bone, a bean, a wild plum stone, a sandstone pebble, a ball of buffalo hair or black mesquite gum, a wooden or stone ball, or, in historic times, a lead bullet. (The hidden-ball game was taken over by many of the white settlers who changed its name to the bullet game. In fact, so many whites became addicted to the game that at one time the Indiana Territory passed a law forbidding the playing of the bullet game).

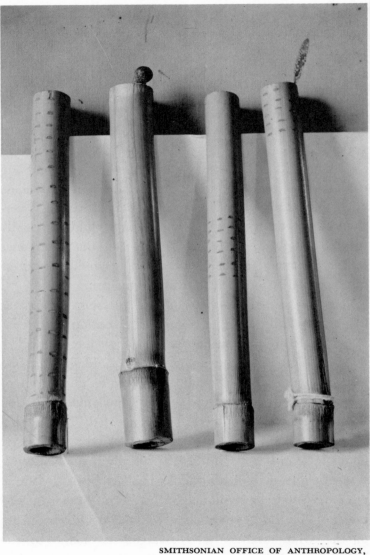

Cane tubes used by Pima Indians in the hidden-ball game.

There were many variations in places to hide the ball. In the Southwest, most players hid the ball in one of four cane tubes or wooden cups, while most Plains and Eastern Indians hid the ball in one of four moccasins.

With us, most games are standardized. That is, there are certain rules and regulations that have to be followed when we play baseball or football or bridge or checkers. These rules apply whether we live in Maine or California, in Alaska or Florida. But that wasn't true with Indian games. Since they had not developed a written language, the Indians couldn't write down the rules for a game. Everything had to be passed on by word of mouth or by sign language. Tribes borrowed games back and forth. Sometimes they picked up all the details about playing a game and keeping score. Just as often they got only a part of the picture and had to make up their own rules. And that's why in a dozen different tribes you might find a dozen different ways to play the same Indian game.

The hidden-ball game was a man's game. Any number of men might play, but generally each side chose one man to do the hiding and another man to do the guessing. While the ball or stick was being hidden, the one hiding it used every sleight-of-hand trick he knew to try to confuse his opponents. Once the ball had been hidden, the concealing side kept "poker faces" so that their expressions wouldn't give away the hiding place. A correct guess on the first try won so many tally sticks, on the second try a smaller number, and a still smaller number on the third. In some tribes, however, a correct guess on the first try merely won that side the chance to do the hiding and scoring took place only as forfeits for wrong guesses. The count was kept with sticks or beans or kernels of corn—ten, twenty, fifty, or one hundred or more. The game continued until one side won all the counters.

There were a number of versions of the hidden-ball game. The Chippewa Indians, for example, hid not one but four bullets under the four moccasins. One of the bullets was specially marked. The players used striking sticks of oak to make their guess. The Chippewa still play this game.

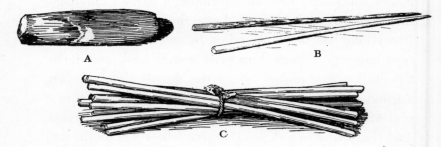

Dakota Indian implements for the hidden-ball game: a) hiding horn; b) pointing sticks; c) counting sticks.

Some Dakota Indians concealed a piece of horn in one of either two, three, or four moccasins, while Delaware Indians are said to have used six moccasins and Navaho Indians as many as eight. Pima and Papago Indians, after dropping a bean into one of four joints of reed, filled the reeds full of sand, then their opponents tried to guess the bean's hiding place. Hopi Indians also filled their four cone-shaped cottonwood cups with sand after hiding a bean or small stone ball in one of them.

Walapai Indians in northwestern Arizona got along without moccasins or cane or wooden tubes. Instead, they

used a 3- or 4-foot long trench dug in loose sand. Holding
the ball, cut out of yucca root, in his left hand, the player
drew his hand along the bottom of the trench, at the same
time piling the sand over the buried hand with his other
hand. When he pulled his hands out, the ball had been left
behind somewhere along the trench. After he divided the
sand in the trench into four heaping piles, the opponents
then had to guess in which of the four sand piles the ball
had been hidden.

Among most Pueblo Indian tribes of Arizona and New
Mexico the hidden-ball game was considered sacred to the
war gods. The cane tubes or cottonwood cups were carved
or painted with symbols of the four directions—north,
south, east, and west. Implements used in this and other
similar games were, and frequently still are, placed upon
many Hopi and Zuni altars and were also used as parts of
ceremonial masks and headdresses. Other Pueblo ceremonial features of the game included songs and chants.

Songs and ceremony also centered around the Chiricahua Apache hidden-ball game. Many Chiricahua
Apaches even went through secret ceremonies to insure
good luck in games and gambling. Like the Navaho and
other Indians, Chiricahua Apaches played the moccasin
game only in winter and only at night. If a person sang
one of the moccasin songs at any other time of the year,
they believed that a rattlesnake would bite him. According
to Apache myth, this was the game played at the beginning
of the world, with birds opposing four-footed animals and
monsters to see whether there should be daylight.

Perhaps the most widely played Indian guessing game
was the so-called hand game, another variation of button,

Two sets of bone cylinders and bundle of counting sticks used by the Umatilla Indians in the hand game.

button. So far, it has been found in nearly a hundred different tribes, ranging all the way from the Great Lakes to California and from Canada to Arizona.

As its name implies, one player concealed in his hands two small wooden or bone cylinders, one plain and one marked by carving or painting or by a cord tied about its middle. The opponents had to guess in which hand the unmarked cylinder was hidden. The number of players varied from two on up, with the players seated on the ground facing each other. In some tribes both men and women played the hand game, while in others only men played it.

The game was also known as the grass game because it was the custom among some California Indians to wrap the two cylinders in bundles of grass.

Just as in the hidden-ball game, the concealer and the other members of his side performed sleight-of-hand tricks, sang songs, swayed their bodies from side to side, and changed facial expressions to try to mislead their oppo-

Paiute Indians in northern Arizona playing the hand game.

nents. The guesser indicated his choice of hands by extending one arm and pointing. If he guessed correctly, the gaming bones went to his side. If he guessed wrong, he lost so many counters. The game was counted with sharpened tally sticks, usually twelve in number but varying from five to sixteen or more, which were stuck in the ground between the players. The game ended when one side had won all the counting sticks.

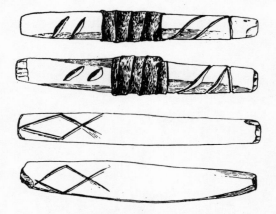

Two sets of carved bones used by the Klamath Indians in the hand game.

Some tribes, like the Kutenai and Klamath, used two identical sets of bone or wooden cylinders, thus eliminating the necessity of passing the cylinders from one side to the other. Such sets were often highly prized for their supposedly lucky qualities and were handed down from one generation to the next.

Nootka Indian children played a team guessing-game that was different from the usual hand game. While one group covered their heads with a blanket or mat, the others passed a small stone from one to the other behind their backs. Then their opponents removed the blanket and tried to guess which one had the stone. If they came up with the right answer, it was their turn to hide the stone. If they were wrong, they lost a point.

Still another Indian guessing-game was the stick game. This was a favorite guessing-game of the California and Northwest Coast Indians. It was also popular among the Crees and Hurons and other tribes of eastern Canada and the United States, where it was sometimes called the straw game.

The stick game was played with a bundle of sticks or reeds, although flat disks were often used along the Pacific Coast. These sticks might number from ten to more than a hundred. They were from 4 to 20 inches long and were frequently painted or carved with distinctive markings. When one of the players divided the bundle into two parts, the object of the game was to guess in which of the two divisions a particular marked stick was hidden or in which division the number of sticks was either odd or even.

As played by the Crees, the bundle of sticks always contained an odd number; one of two known Cree sets holds twenty-five willow splints, the other holds twenty-nine peeled-willow twigs. The game could be played with just two players or with two groups of players. One side began the game by secretly dividing the bundle into two lots. If the opponents guessed which lot contained the even number of sticks, they won. If they picked the odd bundle, they lost.

Huron Indians in Ontario played the game under a slightly different set of rules. An odd number of sticks or straws were mixed and placed on a skin or mat between the players. One of them shoved a pointed bone into the pile and picked up a part of the bundle; his opponent took those that remained. Each player counted his straws, and the one with the odd number won.

Bundle of sticks and dividing stick used by the Sauk and Fox Indians in the stick game.

Sauk and Fox Indians played the same game but used a still different set of rules. One player held the bundle of one hundred and two peeled-willow sticks in his hands and let them fall in a pile. (The number of sticks wasn't always the same; another Sauk and Fox bundle held only fifty-one gaming sticks). The player then divided the sticks with a foot-long dividing stick painted red on the pointed end. The object was to separate an odd number of sticks from the pile, either nine or eleven or thirteen or fifteen and so on. But he had to call out which of these numbers he was trying to separate before putting down the dividing stick. If he succeeded in picking out the number he had chosen, he scored one point. If he missed, the turn went to the next player.

Teton Dakota children in South Dakota played the stick game with a bundle of sumac sticks, one of which was distinguished by a special mark and was called the odd one. With his eyes closed, one of the two players mixed the sticks and separated them into two piles, holding one bundle in each hand. The other player tried to choose the bundle with the odd stick. If he guessed correctly, he won the game. If not, he lost.

The gaming sticks used by the Haida and Tlingit and other Northwest Coast Indians could almost be called works of art. Sets of these sticks were often highly polished and intricately carved or painted or even inlaid with small pieces of abalone shell or ivory. Such sets, consisting of forty-three or forty-nine or fifty-seven or sixty-seven or more sticks, were almost always kept in a leather or skin pouch. And we can be fairly certain that the youngsters were told not to play with them.

The last of our Indian guessing-games, the four-stick game, was played by only a few tribes in Oregon, California, Nevada, and Wyoming—the Klamath, Modoc, Washo, Paiute, and Shoshoni, among others. It may, however, have once had a much wider distribution because archaeologists have dug up similar wooden sticks in prehistoric cliff dwellings in northern Arizona.

The four sticks used in this game were made in pairs. One pair was always slightly longer and slightly larger

Set of carved and plain wooden sticks used by the Klamath Indians in the four-stick game.

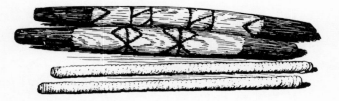

than the other pair. Sometimes one pair was wrapped with buckskin cord while the other pair had painted or burned-in designs.

The game was usually played by two persons who sat on the ground facing each other. One person would hide the four sticks under a mat or blanket or basketry tray and position them in a pattern, in which the sticks were all lying parallel to each other. The other player would then try to guess the relative position of the sticks, whether the larger rods were on the outside or in the middle or if they alternated with the smaller rods. (Can you figure out the six possible combinations of the two large and two small sticks? You can check your answer against the solution given at the end of chapter five.)

TWO-FACED DICE

5

If we see or hear the word "dice," we immediately picture our familiar six-sided cubes of ivory or plastic, with a different number of dots on each face. Today, youngsters as well as adults use dice in a great many games—Backgammon, Monopoly, Clue, Cootie, and a dozen other similar games.

But not all dice are six-sided. You can also have two-sided dice. That was the way most American Indians made their dice, using flat sticks of wood or bone. Since the Indians didn't know how to read or write and couldn't, therefore, put numbers on their dice, they distinguished between the opposite sides by colors or other markings.

Though these two-sided sticks may not look like dice, they serve exactly the same purpose. Instead of using two or more cubical dice, as we generally do, the Indians played with two or four or six or even more two-sided dice. This is the same principle we use in tossing several coins in the air and calling heads or tails. Occasionally, the coins will fall with all heads or all tails facing up. More often, however, they will show a combination of both heads and tails. This is simply the law of chance operating through the algebraic law of combination. Thus, two-sided dice can form the basis for a game of luck or chance equivalent to that of our cubical dice. Actually, games with multiple two-faced dice have been played on most of the world's continents, where cubical dice were known and where they were unknown, as in the New World.

Playing with dice was the favorite sport of North American Indians. Games using multiple two-sided dice have been found in more than one hundred and fifty different tribes from the Atlantic to the Pacific and from Alaska to Mexico.

Indian dice-games are old. Indians have been playing games with dice for at least two thousand years. Archaeologists have dug up numerous sets of two-faced dice in prehistoric ruins in Arizona, New Mexico, Colorado, and Utah. Some are sticks, 3 to 6 inches long, split down the center, with one side flat and the other rounded, and marked with cut lines that perhaps correspond to the dots on our dice. Others are small oval pieces of

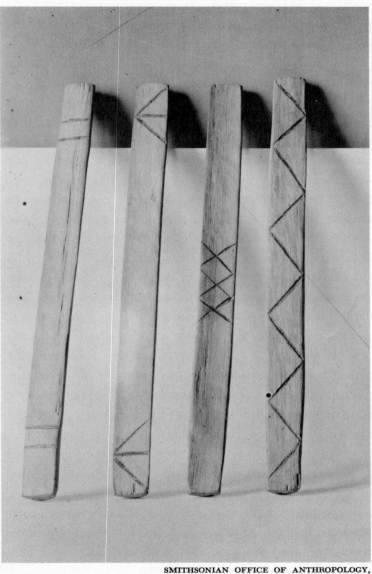

Pima Indian set of four flat wooden dice.

polished bone, an inch or less in length, with similar incised line markings. Some of these dice still show traces of red or black or blue paint on one side. Small wooden dice-cups have also been found in these ancient ruins.

Although the Indians seem to have made most of their two-sided dice out of thin pieces of wood or bone, they used nearly everything that was handy—split canes or reeds or willow twigs, bark, buffalo ribs, beaver and woodchuck teeth, split walnut shells or acorn shells, wild cherry or wild plum stones, grains of corn, mussel or abalone shell disks, or disks of wood or pottery or bone or horn. Some Eskimos even carved ivory or bone dice in the shape of ducks, geese, foxes, and seals.

Indians threw their dice in two ways, either by hand or tossed up in a shallow basket or wooden bowl. The basket-dice game was usually played only by women, while the hand-dice game was commonly played by men.

Throwing dice in a basket wasn't simple. Sometimes the player held the basket near the ground and tossed the dice up in the air, catching them in the basket before they hit the ground. Just as frequently, however, the player merely rapped the basket sharply against the ground, causing the dice to jump around. Sometimes the basket was shaken and the dice thrown out on a blanket or on the ground.

These two-sided dice came in sets. There were anywhere from three to fifteen in a set. Four seems to have been the usual number for most stick-dice, the long pieces of wood or bone thrown by hand, while six or eight was common for the smaller dice tossed up in a basket. Stick-dice were generally long and narrow, about

Set of four carved and painted bone stick-dice used by the
Blackfoot Indians.

an inch in width and ranging from 3 to 23 inches in
length, with most of them averaging between 6 to 9
inches.

Basket-dice, as you would expect, were considerably
smaller, rarely being less than an inch in diameter, yet
seldom reaching 2 inches.

Most dice were blank on one side and the other side
was marked with carved designs of either straight or
zigzag lines or dots. There was no law that said how
dice had to be marked. Each tribe or even each village
could, and generally did, mark its dice as it pleased. Some
tribes, like the Zuni, filled in their incised patterns with
red and black paint and often painted the blank side in
a contrasting color. Other tribes, like the Navaho, sometimes painted one side black and the other black and
white or red and white. When stick-dice were made of
split canes or reeds or of split bone they actually didn't
need carvings or paint to distinguish between the two

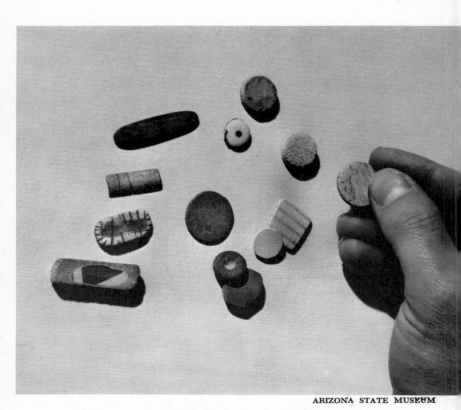

Prehistoric Pueblo Indian stone and bone dice.

faces as one side was always flat and the other naturally rounded. Still, many people didn't seem to think that this was enough because most of these dice were either carved or painted or both.

Frequently the designs on a set of dice were carved or painted alike. Yet just as often they were not. In one set of four Arapaho stick-dice, for example, one side of each die was yellow, with carved notches painted red and green. All the design patterns were different, while the other side of each die was painted plain green. The designs were also different on a set of four Pima stick-dice.

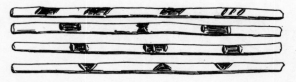

Four Arapaho Indian stick-dice made of painted and carved willow twigs.

In North Dakota, one Hidatsa set of four elkhorn stick-dice had been made in two pairs. Each pair had its own distinct set of patterns of lines and dots. The opposite sides of all four sticks were plain. A set of four Chippewa stick-dice were also marked alike by pairs. In contrast, several sets of Chippewa basket-dice made of bone were all marked alike—plain on one side and painted red on the other side with identical carved cross-hatched designs. Out of ten sets of Pomo stick-dice, six sticks to a set, six of the sets had all of the six sticks in each set marked alike, while three sets had four of the sticks marked alike and two marked differently, and the last set had all six sticks marked differently.

Like some of the Eskimos, the Chippewa, Kickapoo, Cree, and a few other tribes sometimes carved their small wooden or bone basket-dice into the shape of birds or animals or men.

The Indians counted how many marked or plain, flat or rounded, sides of their two-faced dice turned up after a throw. And, where the designs of the marked sides were different, the way each die turned up or down could also affect the count.

There was no fixed rule about counting. Each tribe seems to have made up its own set of rules. Among the

SMITHSONIAN OFFICE OF ANTHROPOLOGY,
BUREAU OF AMERICAN ETHNOLOGY COLLECTION

Chippewa Indian wooden bowl and carved bone dice.

Maricopa Indians, for example, each die of a set of four stick-dice had a different design burned into one face and each design had its own value—25, 15, 6, or 4 points. When the dice were thrown, if any marked side turned up alone, it scored its face value. But two marked sides up only scored 2 points and three sides up 3 points. When the four plain faces were up, the dice went to the opponent. Each player kept score by passing a tally stick or stone along a row of twenty-five shallow pits dug in the ground beside him. Fifty points, twice along the pits, won the game.

The Havasupai Indians used only three stick-dice, white on one side and red on the other. Three white sides up counted as 10 points; two whites and one red up, 2 points; two reds and one white up, 3 points; and three reds up, 5 points.

Basket-dice, usually being greater in number, had a higher and more complicated count. The Cheyenne Indians, for instance, used eight dice, some of whose faces were marked with different designs while others were left blank. Every possible combination of the designs and blank faces gave a different count. The highest possible throw was 200 points and the lowest zero, with the game generally being set at 2,000 points.

The Cayuga Indians in New York used six flattened wild-plum stones, blackened on one side and plain on the other. There were only four winning throws—all plain or all black sides up counting as 4 points and one white or one black counting as 1. When a player made a throw without any count, he lost his turn.

The Seneca Indians in New York had still a different way of counting. They used eight elkhorn buttons, about an inch in diameter, plain on one side and slightly burned on the other to blacken them. One of the players shook the buttons in his hand and threw them out on a blanket. If six turned up the same color, it counted as 2 points; if seven, it counted as 4, and if all eight, it counted as 20. When less than six came up, either plain or black, the throw was passed to the other player. The stakes were fifty or more beans, and the game continued until one of the players had won all of them.

In Montana, the Crow Indians had sets of six dice made of bone or wood or wild plum stones. In each set, three of the dice were circular and three triangular in shape, all

were marked on one side with burnt-in designs. The dice
were tossed by rapping a wooden bowl against the
ground. Scoring was complicated—six plain or marked
dice face up scored 6 points; one marked disk with one
marked triangle, 4 points; two marked disks with one
marked triangle, 3 points; three marked disks, 3 points;
one marked disk, 2 points, three marked disks with two
marked triangles, 1 point.

In most of these stick- and basket-dice games, the score
was kept with counters made of round sticks or twigs,
usually varying in number from ten up to one hundred
and twenty. A game ended when one side won all the
counters.

Still another version of the stick-dice game was played
by the Hopi and Zuni and other Pueblo Indians and by
the Pima and Papago and Havasupai and some of the
other Indian tribes in Arizona and New Mexico. This game
was played on a counting board consisting either of stones
or small pegs set in a circle or square on the ground or a
similar circle or square marked on a large animal hide or
flat stone. It was usually arranged in four divisions of

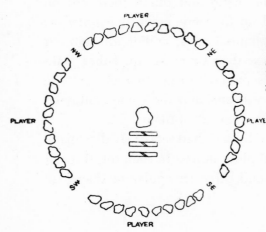

*Counting board of rocks
laid in a circle on the
ground and used by
the western Apaches for
the stick-dice game.*

Havasupai Indian girls playing the stick-dice game.

ten places each (or of four quarters of forty places each), with openings called rivers or gateways at the four corners of the compass. The game was generally played by two to four players, each moving his counter, a stick or a stone, around the circle or square as determined by the throw of the stick-dice. The object of the game was to travel all the way around the course and return to home base, the first to reach there was the winner. In some tribes, if a counter landed on a spot already occupied by the counter of an opponent, the latter piece was "killed" and had to go back to the starting point.

This ancient Indian game is much like the modern game of Backgammon or Parchesi, which we play with cubical dice on a marked board shaped somewhat like a cross. Did we borrow these two games from the American Indians or did they borrow them from us?

Archaeologists don't think either idea is true. Backgammon boards with dice and counters have been uncovered in Babylonian ruins thousands of years old. Played by the ancient Greeks and Romans, the game didn't become popular in Europe until after the tenth century A.D. Parchesi, a game probably originating in India, was brought to Europe and then to America only within the past hundred or more years. Actually, the American Indian form of these games was being played by the Aztecs of Mexico at the time of the Spanish conquest in 1520 A.D. The Spanish or Mexican name for this stick-dice game is derived from the Aztec Indian word *patolli*. From Mexico, the game spread northward, eventually reaching most of the tribes in Arizona and New Mexico but never spreading far beyond their boundaries.

Although dice games were primarily for adults, Indian youngsters seem to have played most of them. The basket-dice game was played by the women and children of most of the Plains Indian tribes, while Havasupai girls played the stick-dice game, which resembles our Parchesi. Chiricahua youngsters played a game similar to our flipping a coin and calling "heads" or "tails." They used a piece of bone with the two sides distinguished from each other by their shape or color. Or sometimes they wet one side and called it "wet" and the other "dry." When a player flipped it in the air, if the side he named showed face up, he kept possession of the bone. If it didn't, the bone changed hands.

Like the hidden-ball game, the stick-dice game was generally thought to be sacred to the Pueblo Indian gods. Gaming sticks were often placed on Pueblo ceremonial altars. Perhaps that is why Indians attribute winning at games of chance to the aid of supernatural powers, while we attribute it to luck.

The six possible combinations of large and small sticks in the four-stick game are:

●● ● ●   ● ● ●●   ● ● ● ●   ●● ● ●   ● ●● ●   ●● ● ●
  1   2   3   4   5   6

GAMES OF SKILL

One or more games of skill were played by nearly every Indian tribe in North America north of Mexico. These were games where an individual's quickness, dexterity, ingenuity, and eyesight counted for more than luck or chance.

One of the most popular of all games of skill was the so-called hoop-and-pole game. It was played, as its name implies, with wooden poles or spears which were thrown at a rolling hoop or ring, the count being determined by the way in which the poles fell in relation to the hoop.

This was a game for men only. In fact, in some tribes, such as the Chiricahua and Mescalero Apaches, women weren't even allowed to go anywhere near the hoop-and-pole ground. To these Indian men, this was a favorite retreat where they could get away from the women and enjoy the free and easy companionship of other men. Even the dogs were kept away from the field when the men were playing.

Still other tribes, however, like the Creeks and some of their Indian neighbors in the southeastern United States, looked on the hoop-and-pole game as a sporting event for the entire village.

They built large playing fields or courts and enclosed them with sloping sides on which the spectators could be seated—prehistoric versions of Yankee Stadium or Candlestick Park.

Like the guessing games and dice games, the hoop-and-pole game was also a major gambling game. So were practically all of the other games of skill. And, like many other Indian games, the hoop-and-pole game was also thought to be sacred or ceremonial in nature. Most tribes had legends or myths telling how the Indians acquired the game from the gods, picking up at the same time as an added bonus a knowledge of buffalo or corn or some other staple food item. Among the Apaches, for example, although any man could play the game, only certain men who knew the songs and ceremony of the hoop-and-pole game made the gaming implements.

There was no one standard version of the hoop-and-pole game. The gaming equipment and the methods of playing and counting varied from tribe to tribe and from

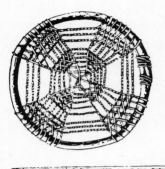

Mandan Indian netted hoop and pole used in the hoop-and-pole game.

region to region. The implements for this game consisted of a target, usually either a hoop or a ring, poles or darts or arrows to throw or shoot at the target, and, sometimes, specially-made counting sticks.

All hoops were more or less circular in shape as they had to be rolled along the ground. But from that point on they showed wide diversity. Hoops could be of almost any size, from 2 inches in diameter among the Sauk and Fox and Paiute to 2 feet or more among the Siouan Dakota Indians. Most, however, averaged from 8 to 12 inches in diameter. The materials from which they were manufactured were equally varied. The most common type of hoop was made of a flexible tree branch or sapling, stripped of its bark, with the two ends tied together with sinew or rawhide to form a circle. Other hoops were made of elm bark (Sauk and Fox Indians), or of bark wrapped with yucca fiber cord (Mohave), or of wood wrapped with buckskin or rawhide (Blackfoot, Navaho, Shoshoni), or of wood wrapped with beads (Ute), or of twigs wrapped with bark (Umatilla, Kwakiutl, Makah), or of corn husks (Hopi). Still other Indians made their rings

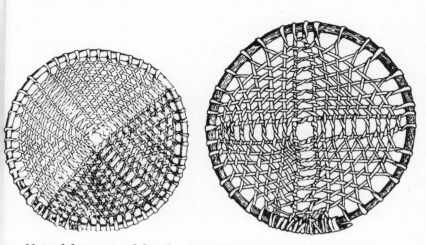

Netted hoops used by the Arapaho and Cheyenne Indians in the hoop-and-pole game.

or hoops out of stone, both with and without holes in them, rough lava on the Pacific Coast (Santa Barbara, Bellacoola, Kwakiutl), or finely finished quartzite or other similar rock in the southeastern United States (Choctaw, Creek, Cherokee).

The opening in many of the wooden hoops was covered with a network of rawhide cords, much like the webbing of a snowshoe or of a tennis racket. Sometimes this network was painted—half red and half blue by the Cheyenne and Arapaho Indians, half red and half black by the Pawnees, and all red by the Chippewas. In some hoops, the opening was simply divided into four quarters by two cords crossing at right angles (New Mexico Pueblos and Omaha Indians), while the Apache Indians reduced this still further to a single cord across the middle of the hoop. But the Apaches also notched the rim of the hoop, as did the Dakotas.

The poles used in this game showed just as much

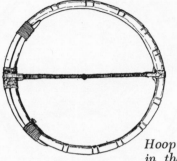

Hoop used by the western Apaches in the hoop-and-pole game.

variation as did the hoops. The Sauk and Fox Indians shot arrows at the rings, while others threw arrows by hand at the rolling hoop. Hopi Indian boys threw foot-long corncob darts made with wooden points and feathered butt ends. The Omaha Indians occasionally used barbed wooden darts, while the Pawnees often put both barbs and crossbars on their darts. The darts of some of the New Mexico Pueblo Indians had thongs which caught in the rings. The Dakota Indians used two short darts attached in the middle by a rawhide cord. Some Omahas and Arapahos also tied their short darts in pairs.

But the most commonly used pole was a simple straight shaft of wood, anywhere from 3 feet long (Arapaho) to 10 to 15 feet long (Apache, Mohave, Walapai). The longer poles were often made in three sections which were spliced together and tied with sinew. The Apaches also marked the butt end of their poles with a series of rings.

Two men normally played the hoop-and-pole game, using a single hoop or ring and two poles, one pole for

Corn-husk ring and feathered corncob darts used by the Hopi Indians in the hoop-and-pole game.

each of the players. Some tribes, such as the Mandan, Hidatsa, and Apache, and most of the Indians of the Southeast, built a regular playing field by smoothing out a stretch of ground and packing the earth down firmly. The Chiricahua Apaches even put a rock in the center and one at each end to mark the boundaries of the 100-foot long field. We don't know the reason for this, but their field could only run in one direction, east and west, with the two players playing from the center toward the ends, first to the east and then to the west.

Hidatsa Indians of North Dakota playing the hoop-and-pole game. After a drawing by Carl Bodmer.

Other tribes generally didn't go to that much trouble and just used the closest level piece of ground that was clear of rocks and brush and other obstacles.

As the game was most commonly played, one of the two players rolled the hoop ahead of them down the course. When it reached a certain distance, both players threw their poles after it, sliding them along the ground. The object was not so much to hit the hoop but to place the pole in such a position that the ring, when it finally stopped rolling, would fall across the pole. This took practice and a good eye for judging distances.

The exact way in which the pole and hoop came together determined the score, which was counted differently by different tribes. To score one point, Maricopa Indians had to throw the pole so that the hoop fell on any part of the pole. To score two points the hoop had to rest on the butt end of the pole. No score was given if the pole went through the hoop. The player who won also won the right to roll the hoop for the next trial. In the Walapai hoop-and-pole game, if the hoop fell over the point of the pole, it counted as 4 points and won the game.

Where hoops with netting or other cords or marks were used, the position of these across the pole usually affected the score. Apache players counted both the value of the particular part of the hoop that touched the pole and also the value of the marks on the butt end of the pole that were enclosed by the hoop. And if a Blackfoot player pierced the center ring of the hoop with his dart, he won the game.

In the Arapaho version of the game, an assistant rolled the hoop for the two players. To score, the Arapaho player had to throw his pair of sticks in such a way that both fell either under or over the hoop. If one was under and one over, the throw counted for nothing. The object of the Pawnee player was to hurl his dart through the still rolling hoop, while Sauk and Fox players tried to shoot their arrows into the spinning ring.

Most of the tribes in the southeastern United States, including the Choctaw, Chickasaw, Cherokee, Creek, and Natchez Indians, played chunkey, their own unique brand of the hoop-and-pole game. Instead of a wooden

*Prehistoric chunkey
stone from Missouri.*

hoop, they used a smooth stone disk 5 or 6 inches in diameter.

Chunkey, and probably also the closely related hoop-and-pole game, is at least as old as the ancient mound builders. Archaeologists have found a number of these chunkey stones in prehistoric-mound and -village sites throughout this southeastern region. At several villages they have even excavated what may have been the remains of old chunkey bowling alleys. Among some of these tribes chunkey stones seem to have been the property of the individual towns and were carefully preserved from one generation to the next.

Although there were several different varieties of chunkey, all made use of a smooth stone disk and two long slender poles. Only two players took part in a game. But there was always a large crowd of onlookers ready and willing to wager everything they owned on the outcome of the game. As in the hoop-and-pole game, the object was for a player to slide his pole and have it stop at the exact spot where the stone stopped rolling. The closest pole scored 1 point, 2 points if it were actually touching the stone. If both poles were equally close, neither player scored. One early account even tells us that the poles were rubbed with bear grease to make them slide better.

The hoop-and-pole game may have been for men only, but plenty of Indian boys also played it. Pawnee Indian boys played with smaller and simpler hoops and poles. So did Dakota and Mandan and Yuma and Klamath and Hopi youngsters. But Blackfoot boys used a larger hoop than their elders, perhaps because the smaller 3-inch hoop was too hard to hit. Chiricahua Apache boys were eager to learn the game, pestering their elders until the latter made smaller sets for them and taught them the rules for counting and keeping score. When the boys were playing, the girls had to stay away from the field.

In the northern snow country, from Montana to Maine, the coming of winter brought out the Indian boys and men for the purpose of playing the snow-snake game. In this game of skill, a dart or spear was hurled along the ice or snow or frozen ground, the object being to see whose dart went the farthest.

For this game you only needed one thing besides snow or icy weather—a specially shaped dart or arrow called a snow-snake. Like most other pieces of Indian gaming equipment, snow-snakes came in all sizes. But they didn't come in all shapes. Snow-snakes were simply round rods of hickory or maple or other hard wood, from 2 to 10 feet

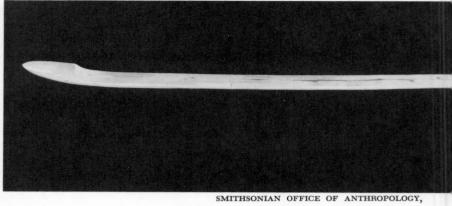

Chippewa Indian snow-snake.

in length, tapering back from a slightly bigger head at the end. To make them glide more easily over snow and ice, they were usually carefully smoothed and highly polished. Sometimes the head end was turned up a little and weighted with horn or bone to increase its momentum.

Many Indians carved the bulbous front end of their snow-snakes to make it look like a real snake's head, even putting in eyes and a mouth. The tail end generally tapered almost to a point, like a snake's, and often ended in a tiny notch for the thrower's finger. Frequently the body was also decorated by burning or smoking it over a fire, giving the wood a brownish color. Sometimes, to give it further ornamentation, a part of the bark was cut

Wooden snow-snake made by the Sauk and Fox Indians.

out in a pattern, perhaps a spiral, and then the stick was smoked before removing the rest of the bark, leaving the spiral design standing out dark against the lighter, unsmoked wood. A man or boy would often put on his personal mark in this fashion, or with paint, so he could readily identify his stick when a number of people were playing.

Like the hoop-and-pole game, this was distinctly a man's game. In some tribes, however, there were special forms for women, as among the Arapaho, Chippewa, and Cree Indians. And, of course, boys played it almost everywhere. The Chippewas even made snow-snakes in different sizes, according to the ages of the boys who were to use them. Where small boys couldn't get their hands on real snow-snakes, they would use makeshift ones of ordinary reeds or weed stalks.

Any open stretch of fairly level land or a lake or river could serve as a playing field for this game, provided only that the ground was either frozen hard or covered with snow and that the lake or river was coated with a thick layer of ice. Many Indians used the snow and ice just as it was. But Chippewa and Seneca players, to make a better and faster track, would drag a log through the snow to form a shallow trench. Sometimes they sprinkled this with water and let it freeze into a smooth, icy runway. In Maine, Penobscot Indians didn't bother to hunt for a log. Instead, they grabbed the nearest boy by the heels and dragged him down a slope to make a path through the snow.

In throwing one of the longer snow-snakes, the player would balance it on his left hand and place the fore-

*Menominee Indian demonstrating how to throw a snow-snake.
From a painting by Mary Irvin Wright.*

finger of his right hand against its back end. A short snow-snake could be thrown by the right hand alone, with the forefinger against its foot and the thumb and other fingers supporting it. The throw was generally, but not always, made underhand.

Since the game's object was to slide the snow-snake along the track as far as possible, a player's success depended not only on his dexterity and muscular strength but also on the balance and finish of his snow-snake. A good player could send his snake shooting down an icy course to a distance of over 300 yards (three times the length of a modern football field). And there are reports of Seneca players sliding snow-snakes 440 yards, a full quarter of a mile! Even small boys could skim their snow-snakes several hundred feet over the snow and ice.

Chippewa boys often threw snow-snakes under and through soft snow. After traveling a long distance beneath the snow, the snake would suddenly jump out and scoot along the top before finally coming to a stop. Cree Indians would sometimes heap up four mounds of loose snow, spacing them about 10 feet or more apart down the course. Then they would hurl their snow-snakes at the first of these artificial barriers and try to make them slide through all four before stopping.

Snow-snake could be played as an individual game or as a team game. In team games, the number of players on a side usually ranged from four to ten. The snake which ran the greatest distance won a point for its team. That same team might win other points as a point was scored for each additional snake which outdistanced all those of the opponents. A game was any agreed-upon number of points. Among the Senecas, this was generally from 7 to 10 points. In a game between two players, the best three out of four throws often determined the winner.

Kiowa Indian feathered bone-slider.

The Cheyenne and Kiowa and some of the other Plains Indian tribes also played a variation of the typical snow-snake game, using winged bones, short pieces of buffalo rib or other bone with feathers stuck in one end. These were either slid along the ice, like snow-snakes, or thrown down and thrust forward against the ice so that they bounced into the air before sliding on down the course.

The Seneca and other Iroquoian tribes played a some-what different snow-snake game called snow-boat. The boat was about 15 inches long, carved out of beech or other hard wood and in the shape of a canoe. The playing field was usually a side hill with an open field below. Each contestant made his own foot-wide trench down the hill and out into the flat by packing down the snow with his feet. The trench was then lined with ice by pouring in water and letting it freeze. The boats them-selves were dipped in water to give them a coating of slippery ice. The boat that slid the farthest won, and other points were counted in the same manner as in the snow-snake game.

Ponca children played a variation of the snow-snake game. Called "slide-a-stick-on-the-ground," this game was played in summer, not in winter. A boy grasped a stick at one end and threw it underhanded along the ground. The boy whose stick slid the farthest was the winner.

Widespread among both Indians and Eskimos was still another game of skill—the ring-and-pin game. In some ways, this is a variation of the hoop-and-pole game and is also somewhat like the well-known European and American cup-and-ball game. An even more descriptive name for it might be "toss-and-catch."

In the ring-and-pin game, the ring or target was tied to a pin or dart by a thong or cord. The object of the game was to catch the ring on the pin or dart.

The ring or target varied from tribe to tribe, both in its shape and in the material from which it was made. Some of the Pueblo Indians used a single hide ring; Algonkian, Siouan, and Athapascan tribes used strings of toe bones of deer; Hupa, Poma, Shasta, and Umatilla Indians used strings of salmon bones; Pima, and Mohave, and Maricopa Indians used pumpkin or gourd rinds; Eskimos used small rodent skulls; Makah and Kwakiutl Indians used seal bones; Paiute and Klamath Indians used balls of tule; Micmac and Passamaquoddy Indians used bundles of pine twigs; and Penobscot Indians used balls of moose hair.

The number of bones or gourd rings on a string ranged from three or four among the Arapaho and Grosventre

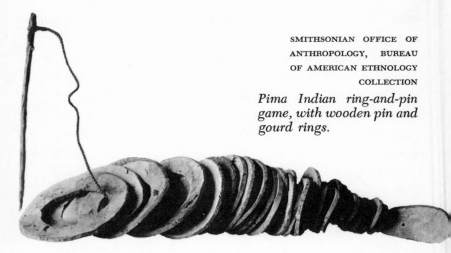

Pima Indian ring-and-pin game, with wooden pin and gourd rings.

Indians to nine among the Crees, with the Pima Indians taking the numerical prize by stringing nineteen gourd rings together. To make these gourd rings, the Indians cut out the center of a squash or other gourd when it was soft. Then they sliced the shell crosswise, forming a dozen or more rings of different sizes. After pressing and drying, these rings became as hard and flat as leather.

Pins, on the other hand, didn't vary much. Most tribes used a pointed piece of wood while a few tribes substituted a sharp bone awl or bone needle. The only exception was the Eskimo, who used both wooden and bone pins as well as carved ivory pins.

Unlike the hoop-and-pole game, the ring-and-pin game was not exclusively for men. Men frequently played it as a gambling game, just as they also bet on the snow-snake game. But women and children probably played the ring-and-pin game for entertainment and

amusement. Two players usually competed against each
other—two boys, two women or two girls, or a young
man and a girl. The latter pairing suggests why the
Cheyenne Indians called it the "love game," the Penobscot Indians the "lover's game," and the Grosventre Indians the "matrimonial game."

The game sounds easy. But swinging a string of bones
or gourd rings or other objects into the air on a short
piece of string and then catching one or more of them
on the sharp point of a stick required skill that only came
with long hours of practice.

(If you don't believe this, try it yourself. You can
make your own ring-and-pin set by stringing half a
dozen hollow sections of chicken or turkey leg bones
on a foot-long strong cord. Tie one end of the cord to
the base of a sharpened piece of wood. On the other end
tie a 3-inch or so square of heavy cardboard to keep the
bones from slipping off the cord. To play, grasp the pin,
point up, with the thumb and forefinger of your right
hand. With your left hand pull the piece of cardboard
back toward your body until the cord and the string
of bones is fairly tight. Then, release the cardboard, at
the same instant giving a quick, upward jerk of your
right hand. This should swing the string of bones outward
and up. All you have to do then is to thrust the point of
your stick forward and try to catch one or more of the
bones on it. Does it still sound simple?)

Scoring in this game was complicated. The more bones
a player caught, the higher his score. Some bones or
gourd rings counted more than others, generally depend-
ing upon their position on the string. And usually the

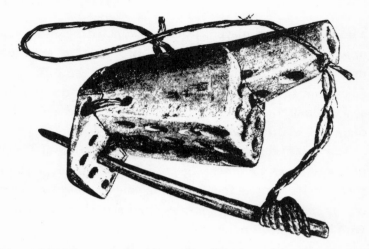

Ivory carving representing a polar bear, used by the central Eskimo in the ring-and-pin game.

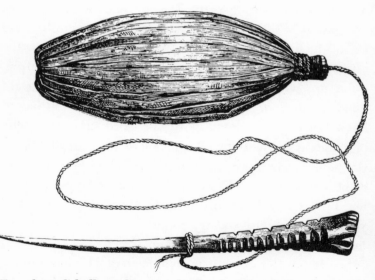

Egg-shaped ball made of rushes and pointed deer-bone pin used by the Thompson Indians of British Columbia in the ring-and-pin game.

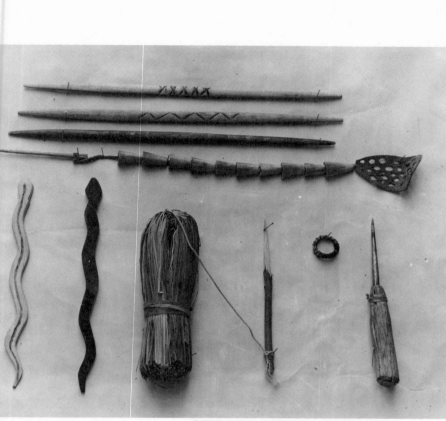

Chippewa Indian gaming pieces. The top two are carved stick dice, while the third is a counting stick. The fourth from the top is a ring-and-pin gaming set. The two small carved snakes are also stick-dice. In the center at the bottom is a wooden pin and bundle of grass for the bunch-of-grass game. At the bottom right is a modern steel awl and a bark ring used in a similar game.

strip of rawhide at the end of the string also had a number of holes in it and catching one or more of these counted for still more points. Where the skull of a rabbit or other rodent was the target, the score was determined by the particular eye or ear socket or other hole that the point of the pin entered.

The Eskimos usually drilled a number of extra holes in their rabbit skulls. They did the same with the ivory copies of rabbit skulls and small models of fox heads and polar bear heads which they carved to use as targets in this game.

Small bundles of grass, tules, or pine twigs were, of course, much easier to spear with the pin. A player usually continued to toss the bundle and catch it until he missed. Since less skill was required, Chippewa Indian girls and youngsters of other tribes were especially fond of playing this version of the ring-and-pin game.

BOWS AND ARROWS
AND DARTS

7

Just as most boys today can hardly wait until they are old enough to get a BB gun or a .22 rifle for their birthday or for Christmas, so did every American Indian boy look forward to the day when he could have his first real bow and arrow.

But Indian youngsters didn't have to wait as long as boys do today. Hopi Indian boys could shoot at a mark almost before they learned how to walk. As soon as a Chippewa boy was able to hold anything in his hands, he was given a tiny bow and arrow and shown how to

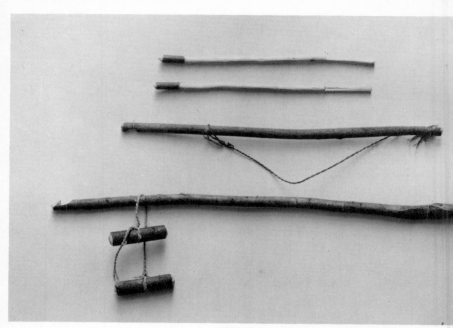

*Chippewa child's bow and arrows, with a child's double-ball
gaming set.*

go through the motions of shooting. A few years later,
when he was five or six years old, he was given a real
bow and real arrows and taught the proper way to shoot.

An Hidatsa Indian boy was given a small bow and
blunt arrows as soon as he was big enough to use them,
about the age of six or seven. At first he would shoot at
targets made of grass or of stuffed rabbit skin, testing
his skill against other boys of the same age. Sometimes
their older brothers would throw stuffed birds into the
air for them to shoot at, offering advice to the younger
boys on how to hit a moving target.

As a boy grew older, his bow became larger and his
arrows more and more pointed. By the age of seven or

eight, Crow and Cheyenne Indian boys had outgrown their stationary and stuffed targets and were ready for bigger game, preferably live. They began to hunt sparrows and blackbirds and other small birds in the sagebrush and thickets close to the village. At first, they missed most of their shots. But now and then they managed to kill a bird. A group of boys would sometimes surround a patch of tall grass and shoot at the mice that scurried out. As their strength and skill increased the boys switched to bigger game—rabbits and gophers and grouse and turkeys.

Hidatsa boys and boys of other tribes also soon learned to put special markings on their arrows so they could identify the rabbits and other animals they had killed.

Once a boy got his first real bow and arrows he spent more time playing with them than with anything else. For the next few years, at least until he reached his teens, he would be absorbed in masculine sports and games and other interests and would have little time for girls.

Archery contests and games were especially popular with boys. One of the simplest forms of Chiricahua and Jicarilla Apache arrow games was shooting for distance, with the winner collecting the arrows of his outdistanced rivals. Chiricahua boys also shot arrows at targets of twisted grass or attempted to shoot arrows through a hole in a yucca plant, while Jicarilla boys shot at a target made of yucca leaves.

In one Blackfoot Indian accuracy game, boys shot at an arrow stuck upright in the ground about 50 yards away. The boy whose arrow was closet to the target

These Chiricahua Apache bow and arrows are said to have been used by Geronimo.

won the arrows of the other contestants. In a second Blackfoot archery contest, called "walking arrow-shooting," one boy shot an arrow on ahead so that it stuck in the ground. The others used it as a target, trying to hit it. After they found out who had won, they didn't go back to the original starting place. Instead, from the site of the first target, a second target arrow was shot on ahead, with all the contestants shooting at it. Arrows were bet on each shot, with the winner taking all.

In one of the favorite Pima Indian target games, each of the players put one of his arrows in a pile. Then, while the players stood in a circle, facing outward, a boy ran around the outside of the circle, dragging a bundle of grass at the end of a long rope. The one who shot his arrow into the bundle of grass as it flew past won the pile of arrows. At the end of the game the best marksman would have the most arrows. The boy who dragged the bundle of grass received a few arrows as compensation for his services. Blackfoot Indian boys had a similar arrow game.

Teton Dakota boys wrapped grass around a piece of bark and threw the oval ball in the air and shot at it, trying to hit it before it landed on the ground.

Pueblo Indian boys used cornhusks as targets, making disks a foot or so in diameter. The one who hit it first, left his arrow there as a target for the others to shoot at. The one who hit it, got to keep the arrow. Zuni boys also used cornhusks as targets, but they hid theirs in the ground. While the other players turned their backs, one boy covered the stick-like bundle of cornhusks with a mound of dirt, at the same time making several other small mounds so no one could tell exactly which mound contained the bundle. After all the players had shot their arrows, largely by guesswork, at the mounds, they went over and pulled their arrows out of the dirt. If one of them had managed to hit the bundle of cornhusks, it came out stuck on the head of his arrow.

In the Pawnee and Ponca tribes, one boy would shoot an arrow 40 or 50 yards ahead so that it fell flat on the ground. The other boys, in turn, would try to shoot so that their arrows would fall directly across the first arrow. Whoever managed to accomplish this feat would win all the arrows that had been shot.

Indian youngsters also played a lot of games with just arrows. Apaches and Eskimos and some Pueblo Indians tossed their arrows at an arrow on the ground so that they fell one across the other. In still another version, one Pueblo Indian boy would throw an arrow along the ground, point forward, 10 feet or so in front of him. All the others would then slide their arrows at it, the aim of the game being to have the feathers of their arrows touch the feathers of the arrow on the ground. Chiricahua Apache boys played a similar sliding-arrow game, as did Comanche boys.

Many Indians also like to play dart games, throwing feathered darts at targets. Pueblo Indian darts were slender wooden sticks pointed at one end and poked through the central core of a corncob so that their points stuck out a few inches from one end. Attached to the other end were a couple of hawk tail-feathers to aid in guiding its flight. The target might be a ball of yucca fiber or a ring of cornhusks, and the one who hit it the greatest number of times would win the game. Maricopa Indian boys also played a similar dart game, while Zuni Indians threw short wooden sticks with two fluffy feathers at the butt end.

Like many of the other Indian games, bow-and-arrow games served to train youngsters for their future adult lives as hunters and warriors. According to one of the early nineteenth-century explorers, Mandan Indian boys were taught the art of war in sham battles. A hundred or more boys between the ages of seven and fifteen were divided into two armies, each headed by an older man, one of the experienced warriors, as a leader and teacher. After shooting at each other with miniature bows and blunt arrows, the boys returned to the village and put on a scalp dance with imitation scalps before an admiring audience of girls.

LET'S PLAY BALL

8

The North American Indians had four major ball games—racket, in which the ball was tossed with a netted racket; shinny, in which the ball was struck with a bat or club; double ball, commonly known as the woman's game, played with two balls or blocks of wood tied together and tossed with a stick; and the ball race, in which a ball or stick was kicked with the foot.

Curiously, in none of these games was the ball ever touched with the hand, as in our modern games of baseball, football, and basketball. It was either batted with a club or racket held in the hand or kicked with the foot. In fact, the rules expressly prohibited touching the ball with the hands.

The racket ball-game was the favorite athletic game of most of the eastern Indians from Hudson Bay to the Gulf of Mexico. This game could be called their national pastime, just as baseball is with us.

Archaeologists think that some of the tribes in the Southeast, perhaps the Creeks or Cherokees, were the originators of this game a thousand or so years ago. From there, it spread up the Mississippi into parts of the Plains and up the Atlantic Coast into Canada. In historic times, incoming European settlers picked up the game from New England and Canadian Indian tribes. Now it has become the Canadian national game under the name of lacrosse and is also played in many of our colleges.

The game of racket or lacrosse was primarily a man's game. Unlike most of the games we have been talking about which were played by only a small number of people, lacrosse was generally a tribal or intertribal contest, with players often running up into the hundreds.

The ball players of the southern tribes used two rackets, while their northern neighbors used only one. These rackets were made of smooth sticks of hardwood, from 2 to 4 feet in length, with one end curved or bent into a small hoop about 4 to 5 inches in diameter. This hoop was crisscrossed with a number of rawhide cords which formed a netted pocket for the ball.

The ball itself was usually from 3 to 4 inches in diameter, just big enough to fit into the netted pocket of the racket. It was made either of a rounded piece of wood or of buckskin stuffed with deer hair (Cherokee) or of moose hair

Iroquois lacrosse rackets.

(Penobscot) or of rabbit hair (Shoshoni) or of mountain-sheep horn shavings (Nootka). The wooden ball seems to have been the older and possibly the original form. Chippewa Indians used to make their wooden lacrosse balls by repeatedly charring a knot of wood and scraping off the charred area until the ball was the right size and shape.

One of the remarkable features of this game, as well as of most of the other Indian ball games, was the extreme length of the playing field, ranging anywhere from 500 feet on up to a mile or more. At either end of the field were two posts or poles which marked the goals, although the Miami and Chippewa Indians sometimes used single posts.

At the beginning of the game, the two teams lined up near the center of the field, every player armed with a racket in each hand (only one racket, of course, among the Iroquois and other northern tribes). The ball was thrown up between the two teams and the players tried to catch it between their two rackets or to bat it toward the opposite goal. The object of the game was to throw the ball or carry it between the opposing team's goal posts. Players could run with the ball or hit it, but they couldn't touch it with their hands. They could try to get it away from whoever had it. And there was no law that said they couldn't use any means short of murder.

Lacrosse was no game for weaklings. To the Indians it offered excellent training for war, developing teamwork and skill in running and warding off blows. In its native form, as played by the able-bodied men of a tribe, it was a rough game. Rackets could be, and usually were, used as clubs. Scrimmages were violent and generally bloody. Broken heads and dislocated joints and broken bones were frequent occurrences. Nor was it uncommon for players to be killed. In one Choctaw game played only last century, five men were crippled, two of whom later died.

In the Southeast, lacrosse was not only an athletic event but was also a ceremonial contest matching village against village, tribe against tribe. The big games between two Cherokee towns are comparable to today's opening-day baseball game, with the President of the United States throwing out the first ball. Only in lacrosse, a medicine man usually put the ball in play.

Preparations for a big game might go on for months in advance. Players trained as faithfully and as hard as today's college and professional baseball and football players do. Certain foods were tabooed, such as rabbits, which might make the players timid and witless. Dances and ceremonies held before the game were supposed to bring strength and success to the team through the aid of the supernatural powers.

Like most other public Indian games, lacrosse provided an excellent opportunity for the hundreds and thousands of spectators to bet heavily on the outcome of the game.

Lacrosse was not a game for children. But, knowing youngsters, it is highly probable that Indian boys did play modified versions of it whenever they had the chance.

A second ball game, shinny, was almost universal among the Indians of North America. This was essentially a woman's game. But it was also played by men alone (Assiniboines, Mohaves, Makahs and Walapais), by men and women alone (Sauk and Foxes, Poncas, and some of the Pueblos), by men and women together (Sauk and Foxes), and by men against women (Crows).

As in lacrosse, the ball could not be touched with the hand. But it could be batted with a stick or kicked with the foot.

The bat was a 2- to 4-foot stick of wood, curved at the lower or striking end. The shape was somewhat like that of a modern golf club or ice-hockey stick. In fact, you might call this game Indian ice hockey as it was sometimes played on the frozen ice of rivers or lakes. The ball was usually made of wood on the Pacific Coast and in the Southwest and of hair-stuffed buckskin in the Plains and the East. The Arapaho, Chippewa, Pawnee, Cheyenne,

Buckskin ball and curved wooden stick used by young Chey-
enne Indian girls to play shinny.

and other tribes often painted or carved designs on their
sticks and also painted designs on the buckskin covers of
their balls. These were usually sacred symbols that were
supposed to bring good fortune to the players.

The shinny playing-field was long, from 200 to 400
yards, although one Ponca field is said to have been a
mile long and half a mile wide. Goals were usually two
posts or stakes at the ends of the field. Two blankets
spread out side by side on the ground served as goals for

A western Apache
buckskin-covered
ball.

the Crows; a single post was the goal for the Menominee, Poncas, and Omahas; and lines drawn across the ends of the field were the goals for the Navaho, Eskimo, Makah.

Any number might play on a side. Among the Comanches and Assiniboines, ten women or girls formed the usual team, while Walapai and Blackfoot teams consisted of from seven to fifteen men. An Omaha or Ponca team, however, might run as high as thirty to fifty players.

To begin play in a game of shinny, an umpire, often a medicine man, placed the ball in the middle of the field, either covering it over with dirt, as among the Walapai and Hopi, or leaving it in a hole in the ground, or tossing it up in the air. At the medicine man's signal, while some of the players guarded their respective goals, the others rushed toward the center of the field and tried to bat or kick the ball toward their opponents' goal. Every time one side succeeded in driving the ball between the other side's goal posts or across their goal line a point was scored. In Ponca games, the first team to score 4 goals won the game.

Most Pueblo Indian tribes played shinny. Among the Hopis, the older and bigger boys and girls played separately from the younger children. The bigger children used larger clubs and longer courses than the younger ones. Some New Mexican Pueblo Indians, men, women, and children, played shinny on the ice in winter.

Shinny may not have been as bloody and dangerous a game as lacrosse. But it was still a rough game, even when played by women and children. In the excitement of the game, a player would often get hit across the shins or clubbed over the head.

Most Indian tribes also played the game of double ball. Except for a few tribes on the Pacific Coast this was strictly a woman's game.

You might call double ball a faster and more difficult variation of shinny. The game was played with two balls or blocks of wood and a curved stick with which the balls were thrown.

The balls were usually made of buckskin, and they were fastened together with a rawhide cord a foot or so long. The Sauk and Foxes and other Algonkian tribes often weighted their balls with sand. Maricopa Indians used strips of leather or willow bark about 9 inches long, with a heavy knot at either end. The Chippewa, Papago, Hupa, and Klamath Indians made their balls out of short cylinders of wood, or bone, tied together with a rawhide cord. The sticks, made of saplings, generally tapered to the end and were slightly curved. They varied in length from 2 to 6 feet. The goals or bases were posts among the Chippewa, and piles of dirt among the Omaha. They were from 200 yards (Maricopa) to a mile (Cree) apart.

Any number of women could play the double-ball

SMITHSONIAN OFFICE OF ANTHROPOLOGY,
BUREAU OF AMERICAN ETHNOLOGY COLLECTION

Pima Indian double ball.

game. But the usual number on a side was from five to six up to ten.

The game started with a referee or another individual tossing the double ball into the air in the center of the field between the two teams. The players tried to catch the double ball on their sticks and pass it to a teammate toward the goal. The object was to carry or throw the double ball the length of the field and wrap the cord around the post or drive the ball between the goal posts. The double ball could only be carried or tossed with the stick. It could not be touched with the hands or kicked. If a Pima player, for example, touched the double ball with her hands, she was immediately thrown out of the game.

Chippewa girls were taught double ball at an early age. They were given smaller gaming implements and, to make it easier for them to catch and hold the cord between the double ball, their sticks were sometimes notched near the end.

Maricopa women played double ball throughout the year. However, this wasn't the case everywhere. Paiute women played the game in spring and summer while Klamath women played it only in summer.

The fourth major American Indian ball-game was the ball race. Only the tribes in the Southwest and in parts of California and northern Mexico seem to have played this game. This was a game in which two individual players or two teams kicked a ball or stick around a course and back to the starting point.

The ball used in this game was small, usually not more than 3 or 4 inches in diameter—about the size of a cro-

Pima Indian kicking balls. The first and third from the left are of wood and stone, respectively, while the other two have been covered with mesquite gum.

quet ball. Maricopas, Monos, and Hopis, among others, used balls of stone while Papagos, Cocopas, Mohaves, and Yumas used balls of wood; Pimas used both. Navahos and Zunis kicked a 4- or 5-inch cylinder of wood. Walapai Indians, perhaps thinking of their bare toes, sometimes made a ball out of yucca root covered with gum or pitch. Pima Indians tried to soften their stone or wooden balls by dipping them in mesquite gum. So did some Hopis, coating a ball of hair with pinyon gum.

Kicking a stone ball or wooden stick with the bare foot and at the same time running as fast as you can sounds difficult. But Pima Indians say that they can run faster with than without the kicking ball. Two boys will run long distances together, kicking the ball so that it is almost constantly flying through the air. The ball isn't kicked with the end of the toes. The kicker tries to push his toes under the ball or stick and lift it into the air with his instep much the same way as many of our barefooted Hawaiians kick a football today.

The ball race or kick-stick race could be played by two

men or by two teams of from three to six or more players each.

Kick-ball racing was the most popular Hopi outdoor game. In this game, a runner ran barefoot, kicking a ball in front of him over a cross-country course of 20 or 30 miles. Two teams would play, with four or five runners to a side. Each team had its own ball, which was either a stick of wood or a small stone ball. One member of each team would start the game by kicking the ball down the course. It would then be kicked by any of the other team members as they raced after the ball. A good kicker could send the ball or stick about 20 or 30 yards or more. If the ball got tangled up in brush or landed in a hollow or a bunch of rocks, it might cost several lusty kicks and a battered toe or two to get it back on the track. Men generally would come home from a race with their insteps sore and swollen. Young men would practice all year to condition themselves for these races.

Hopi kick races took place in spring and early summer when, according to their belief, the rolling of the ball would start the streams racing down the gullies and canyons.

To aid one side against another by trying to slow down or impede the opposing kickers, magic was often used. Maricopa shamans, for example, in ball races between Maricopas and Pimas, would draw a line across the path of the Pima runner to make him think it was a deep, impassable canyon.

Like their not-too-distant neighbors, the Hopis, the Zuni Indians were equally fond of kick-stick races. They usually painted bands of red around their kicking sticks

Carved wooden sticks kicked by the Zuni Indians in ceremonial races.

or carved the bark into distinguishing marks. And like the Hopi ball race, the Zuni kick-stick race was a team race, run over a tough, 25-mile course, with such natural hazards as sand and rocks and brush and hills.

Almost the entire male population, from boys of five or six to men of forty, took part in the sport. Training began at childhood. At the age of four or five, a Zuni youngster would be playing at kicking a stick around the yard. Within another two or three years, he would practice kicking the stick as he came and went from the cornfield where he had been engaged all day in frightening off the crows. A few years later, he and boys his age were organizing their own kick-stick races, patterning them after the races of their fathers and older brothers, but on a smaller scale.

Most Zuni kick-stick races, like those of the Hopis,

had a ceremonial significance. They might be called prayers for rain to water the earth so that the crops might grow.

Lacrosse, shinny, double ball, and the kick-ball or kick-stick race weren't the only Indian ball games. Plains Indian youngsters, as well as children and adults of other tribes, played other games with stone or buckskin-covered balls or with the blown-up bladders of deer and buffalo and other animals. Some of these games may be old; the ones that seem to combine parts of our own games of baseball and football may have been picked up from the early white traders and settlers during the past century or two.

One Southwestern game that may be old resembles present-day bowling or quoits—throwing or rolling a stone ball or disk at a target. Some of the Pueblo Indians pitched a thin sandstone disk or flat stone at a corncob, while Pimas and Mohaves tried to toss round stones into a hole in the ground. Numbers of similar stone and clay disks that have been found in ancient ruins in Arizona and New Mexico may have been used in just such a game.

In the southeastern United States, archaeologists think they may have uncovered a special type of prehistoric bowling alley, one in which stone disks shaped like the chunkey stones were used. In one mound site in Georgia, they found three hard-baked clay runways about 20 feet long. At one end were a series of stone-lined compartments, three on one side and one at the end. A log embedded in the earth formed the side of the runway opposite the small compartments. Tests made with some of these stone disks with beveled edges showed that, when rolled down the runway with the proper control, the stones would frequently curve into one or the other of these compartments. We don't know if these were ancient Indian bowling alleys, but they could well have been.

One Indian ball game that does appear to be old is that of juggling two or more balls in the air at the same time. It was played by at least a dozen tribes, from the Eskimos in Canada to the Maricopas in Arizona.

Maricopa Indian youngsters juggled two, three, or four small wild gourds or round stones or clay balls. Zuni women made balls of red clay about the size of hens' eggs for the boys to juggle. Ute and Shoshoni Indian children also liked to juggle balls of red clay or mud. Some Shoshoni women even made fancy sets of smooth stone juggling balls, painting them in blue or red or white. They usually juggled three balls at a time. Some Eskimos juggled as many as five pebbles at the same time.

Nearly two thousand years ago a major feature of most Mayan ceremonial centers or cities was a large ball court built of stone. Though most of the excavations of these courts have been in Mexico and Central America, the homeland of the Mayas, Zapotecs, and Aztecs, there is some proof that North American Indians also played this ball game.

These paved courts were up to 500 feet long and 200 feet wide, with high side walls. Into the middle of each long facing wall was set a stone ring, the opening of which was perpendicular to the ground, not horizontal as is the hoop in our basketball courts.

This was a ceremonial ball-game, witnessed by hun-

An oval-shaped ball court used by prehistoric Hohokam Indians in southern Arizonia.

Native rubber ball used by the prehistoric Indians in southern Arizona.

dreds, perhaps thousands, of spectators. We can't be certain about the rules of the game. There were two competing teams of from one to fifteen players each. They used a solid but bouncy rubber ball. The object of the game was to drive the ball through one of the rings. To keep the ball in the air the players could use their hips, thighs, or elbows but not their hands or feet. If a player managed to put the ball through the ring, all the spectators took to their heels, since ancient custom said that the lucky player could take all their clothing and jewelry, provided, of course, that he or his friends could catch them.

Like lacrosse, this was a rough game. The players often suffered severe bruises and sometimes fatal injuries. Leather padding may have been used to protect the hips. Most archaeologists seem to think that the players wore huge stone yokes on their hips at pregame ceremonies and possibly during the game itself.

Similar but smaller ball courts have also been found throughout southern and north central Arizona. Built of earth and clay instead of the stone of the Mayan courts, these were used by prehistoric Indians well over a thousand years ago. Two rubber balls, perhaps a pair that saw use in some of these games, were actually found in an ancient village site in southern Arizona.

These Arizona ball courts were in ruins by the time the first Spanish explorers pushed their way into the area in the sixteenth century. And the Indians who played on these courts had either vanished or moved in with some of their Indian neighbors in Arizona and New Mexico.

CAT'S CRADLES AND OTHER STRING FIGURES

9

Many youngsters probably have, at one time or another, taken an endless loop of string and made a "cat's cradle" or other type of string figure by looping and crossing the string between the fingers.

What you may not know is that the trick of weaving patterns with string upon the fingers is a game that has been played by millions of youngsters and grownups all over the world for thousands of years. It was especially popular among the so-called primitive peoples. And it is still played in many countries today.

We call this game played with string "cat's cradle" because the first figure that most Americans and Europeans learned how to make looked like a cat's cradle. Other people have other names for their version of the game. Some Indonesians call it the "ladder game," while Chinese call it "sawing wood" and Navaho Indians "continuous weaving."

The string game seems to have originated somewhere in eastern Asia, possibly in ancient China. From there it spread southward throughout the rest of Asia and Indonesia to the Polynesian Islands and Australia, westward to Europe, and northeastward across the Bering Strait to North America. Perhaps some late-coming Eskimos brought the game with them when they migrated from Siberia to Alaska and northern Canada.

Playing games with string was, and still is, one of the favorite pastimes of children and adults in a great many North American Indian tribes.

Like most other Indian games, weaving with string also had its magical or ceremonial interpretations. In Chapter 1, we mentioned that the Navaho Indians accounted for the web-like patterns in the string game by saying that the ancient Spider people taught the game to their ancestors. The Zuni Indians have the same tradition, explaining the game as the netted shield of the War Gods, taught to the latter by their grandmother, the Spider. Some Eskimos play cat's cradle in the fall of the year in order to catch the sun in the meshes of the string and prevent it from disappearing below the southern horizon. The Nootka and some other peoples believed that children should not make string figures when their

fathers were out fishing or harpooning sea mammals because their fathers' fingers might get caught in the fish
or harpoon lines.

The Navaho Indians have an even stronger prohibition
against weaving with string at certain times of the year.
They believe that the Spider people taught them how to
play the game on the condition that string figures were
to be made only in winter, when the spiders and snakes
were asleep and could not see the figures. The following
true story illustrates just how strong this belief is. During
the late nineteenth century, a rattlesnake almost bit a
young Navaho boy. When he told his mother about it,
she said, "That's what you get for making string figures
in the summer."

String figures are made with a piece of string about 6
feet long. When the two ends are tied together, they
form a single continuous loop about 3 feet long. Some
Indians used a rawhide thong of deerskin, others a cord
of yucca fiber or other plant fiber, still others used cords
of cedar bark or human hair. Pueblo Indians who grew
cotton were able to make their strings out of cotton cords.
This 3-foot loop is stretched between the two hands
which are held out, with the palms facing each other
and the fingers extended upward. The original loop is
then so manipulated with the fingers that a number of
secondary loops cross from the fingers of one hand to
the fingers of the other to form a figure or design. It is
surprising what an almost infinite variety of figures can
be made with just a simple loop of string.

Indian youngsters liked to play the string game. It was
a game that except for certain tribal prohibitions could

Navaho Indian with a string figure he has just finished making.

be played anytime, anywhere, indoors or out, day or
night, good weather or bad. And it could be played by
one individual or by a dozen. All that was needed was a
piece of string. Boys and girls would spend hours pa-
tiently working out the different loops and twists and
turns of old, familiar patterns or trying to form new designs.

For some figures the two hands weren't enough. So
Indians used their teeth and toes and knees and even
sticks and stones and anything else that was handy to
help hold strings in place while they worked. For that
reason, two persons were sometimes partners, working
together on the same pattern, on the principle that four
hands are better than two. Or two persons could play
string games together, the left hand of one and the right
hand of the other forming one figure while the other
two hands were making an entirely different pattern.
In fact, any number of individuals could play together
in the same way.

Some of you may think that cat's cradle is a girl's game.
But it was far from that for American Indians and for
most other peoples of Asia and Indonesia and Australia.
The making of string figures furnished recreation for young
and old Chiricahua Apaches, both male and female. And
that was the way it was with nearly all other American
Indian tribes. To cite one example, in the late nineteenth
century an old Eskimo man in Alaska entertained a snow-
bound anthropologist for over an hour by weaving between his extended hands a never-ending succession of
intricate string figures with his sinew cord.

The object of most string games was to form final

patterns, representing definite objects such as birds or animals or houses. (An active imagination may be needed to see some of these supposed birds and animals.) These figures usually had names, similar to our cat's cradle. Some string games, however, were tricks,

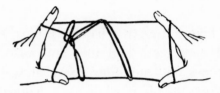

Eskimo string figure of a deer.

with a surprise ending. That is, after a design was finished, the entire loop might be withdrawn from the hands by some simple movement. One figure that the Chiricahua Apaches made could be completely collapsed by a quick twist of the hands. Still other string games might be called catches, since, by pulling certain strings, the hand or the fingers could be unexpectedly caught in a running noose.

Some of the designs that Indian youngsters and adults made were simple, while others were extremely complicated. (Actually, perhaps the world's most complicated string figures come from what have been called the world's most primitive peoples, the Australian aborigines.) Maricopa Indians made figures of turtles, while both Zuni and Navaho Indians made lightning designs, Pueblo Indians butterflies, Pomo Indians hummingbirds, and Eskimos polar bears and walrus heads. Some Indians even made moving figures. A favorite Eskimo

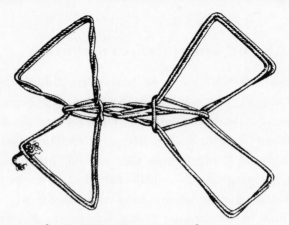

Maricopa string figure representing a turtle.

Zuni Indian string figure of lightning.

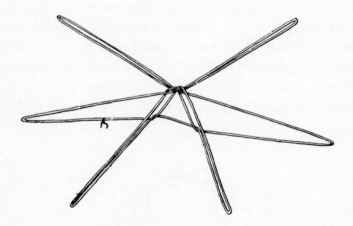

Cochiti Indian string figure representing a butterfly.

figure was the design of a reindeer which, by moving the fingers, was made to look as though the reindeer was running downhill. Another Eskimo pattern illustrated two reindeer fighting. The Klamath Indians also made a number of string figures that moved, including "a little boy carrying mud," "a little fish that hides in the mud," and "two coyotes running from each other."

Some of the simpler string figures are practically universal, and are found all over the world. Others are unique in that they occur only in certain areas or among certain tribes. Still others have been found in several widely separated localities. For example, the Cherokee Indian design called "Crow's feet" is the same as a well-known string game found in such places as Scotland, Ireland, England, Africa, and Australia.

String figures are easy to make. Anyone can learn how to make simple patterns with little or no practice. Yet they can also be exceedingly difficult. It is almost impossible to look at a completed design, like the Eskimo "hills and ponds," for example, and then try to make the identical pattern. Without a knowledge of the exact steps to follow, a person won't know how to start. And that's important, because all string games begin with an

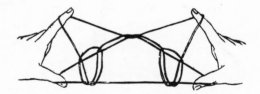

Eskimo string figure showing "hills and ponds."

opening. That is, the loop of string is arranged on the two hands in a certain definite position. And, although many string figures begin with the same opening, there are just as many that don't.

Let's take a look at one of the most typical of these openings and then see how to create an Indian string figure. If you will get a 6-foot length of string or cord and tie the ends together to make an endless loop, you can follow the diagrams and directions and construct the identical pattern we are going to make—a Jicarilla Apache Door.

Although a 6-foot cord is about right for most children, a longer cord will probably produce better results for older youngsters and adults. For more elaborate figures an even longer cord may be necessary. In fact, some of the South Sea Islanders use cords up to 16 feet in length for their intricate designs.

First, put the loop of string on your two hands as shown in Figure 1. Bring your hands together and put

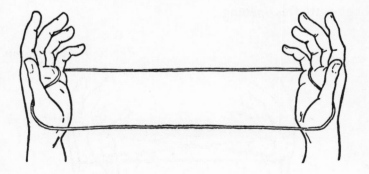

Figure 1. Opening step in beginning the string figure called a "Door" by the Jicarilla Apaches.

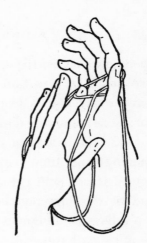

Figure 2. Second step.   Figure 3. Third step.

your right first (index) finger up under the string crossing the left palm (Fig. 2), drawing the loop out on the
back of the finger by separating the hands. Repeat the
process with your left first finger (Fig. 3), and separate
the hands. The pattern should now look like that in Figure 4. This pattern is what experts in string figures call
Opening A. A great many American Indian string figures
begin with this opening.

Figure 4. Fourth step.

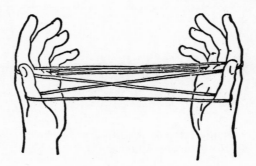

Now we are ready to make the figure that Jicarilla Apaches call the Door. With the right thumb and first finger lift up the loop around the left first finger and let it drop down on the back of the left wrist. Do the same with the loop on the right first finger, letting it drop on the back of the right wrist. Separating the hands and drawing the strings tight should make the design look like Figure 5, with a loop on each thumb and each little finger, as well as a loop on each wrist.

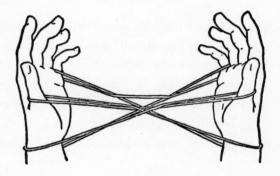

Figure 5. Fifth step.

Next, with the right thumb and first finger pick up the left little finger string nearest you (not the whole loop) and pass it between the left first finger and thumb and let it go. With the right thumb and first finger pick up the looped string on the far side of the left thumb (not the whole loop) and pass it between the left ring and little fingers. Using the left thumb and first finger, repeat this process with the strings on the loops of the little finger and thumb of the right hand. You should now have a loop on each wrist and two strings crossing each palm as in Figure 6.

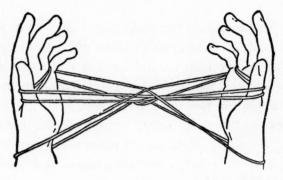

Figure 6. Sixth step.

Keeping all these strings in place on both hands, with the left hand tightly grasp all the strings where they cross in the center of the figure and pass all of them together from left to right between the right first finger and the right thumb (Fig. 7). Leave these strings there and, with the left thumb and first finger, take hold of the two loops already on the right thumb and draw them

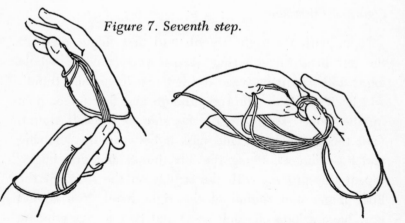

Figure 7. Seventh step.

Figure. 8. Eighth step.

gently over the tip of the right thumb (Fig. 8). Now, still holding these loops, let the collection of strings lying between the right finger and thumb slip over the right thumb to the palm of the hand. This leaves the right thumb entirely free. Without untwisting the two original right-thumb loops, which you are still holding, replace these loops on the right thumb exactly as they were before (Fig. 9). Pull the hands apart and draw the strings tight.

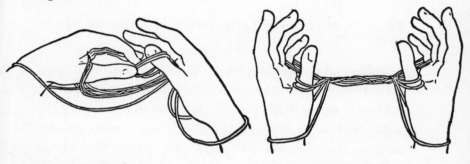

Figure 9. Ninth step.   *Figure 10. Tenth step.*

Repeat this last entire process on the left hand. When you get through, you should have a loop on each wrist, two twisted loops on each thumb, and two twisted loops on each little finger, as in Figure 10.

With the right thumb and first finger lift the left wrist loop from the back of the left wrist up over the tips of all the left fingers and let it fall on the palm side of the hand. With the left thumb and first finger lift the right wrist loop up over the tips of all the right fingers and let it fall on the palm side. Then keeping the loops on the thumbs and little fingers, separate the hands and draw the strings tight.

Your completed string figure should now look like the one illustrated in Figure 11, which the Jicarilla

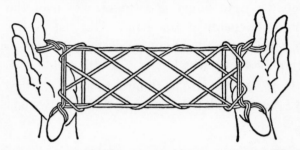

Figure 11. The completed string pattern of the Jicarilla Apache Door.

Apaches call an Apache Door. Navaho and Pueblo Indians make the same string figure but call it by different names.

Once a figure is completed, the problem of getting the string back to its original condition arises. Unless you are careful, the chances are good that you will end up with a tangled mass of cord. With most string figures, the best way to avoid this is to place the completed figure on your lap or on a table top and draw apart the straight strings at the top and bottom of the pattern. The figure should then come undone and leave you with your original long loop of string.

The Apache Door is only one of hundreds of string figures that the Indians and Eskimos made. If you want to make others, look into some of the references listed in the bibliography at the end of this book. Or you can try your luck at creating your own designs.

TELL US A STORY

10

American Indian youngsters didn't have today's book-stores and libraries filled with picture books and story books. But they had something almost as good—story-tellers.

Many winter nights would find the children gathered around the campfire, listening to a storyteller. Some of these stories were the myths and legends of the tribe telling of the creation of the world and of the origins of fire and plants and animals and of all the events leading up to that present time. Some were stories about the ancient gods and other supernatural beings and the miraculous things they did.

Favorites of most youngsters, however, were the stories of the pranks of tricksters. Often, in the evening, some older person would regale the children with humorous tales of the adventures and misadventures of such characters as Coyote and Raven and Mink. These stories were from a long-ago era when birds and animals talked. In fact, the Mescalero Apaches and other Indians would sometimes picture their Coyote trickster as an animal, sometimes as a human being. Frequently the Indians also portrayed him as a Dr.-Jekyll-and-Mr.-Hyde character. On the one hand he was a culture hero, a teacher or savior, bringing benefits to man. Yet, at the same time, he was shown as a greedy old reprobate, ready and willing for the worst kind of mischief.

Old Man Coyote of Crow Indian mythology is an illustration of this curious combination of good and evil. Back when the whole world was covered with water, Old Man Coyote had water birds dive for mud. After three of them failed, the fourth brought up a little mud which Old Man Coyote magically expanded to form the earth. Later he created man and instructed him in all the various arts and crafts. Then the Mr. Hyde side of his character came to the surface. Coyote wandered around the world, cheating others to obtain food, stooping to the meanest of tricks to gain his ends, and even occasionally getting tricked himself. In this role, he was anything but an admirable individual.

The antics of these culture-hero tricksters—Coyote of the Plains and Southwest, Raven of the Northwest Coast, and Rabbit or Hare of the Eastern Woodlands—were an unending source of amusement for youngsters. And, like many of our fairy tales and Mother Goose rhymes, these stories often pointed out a moral lesson to Indian boys and girls.

There were also myths about the stars and about the origin of sacred rituals. There were stories about birds and animals and mythological creatures. There were war stories and mystery stories and love stories. There were tales of the heroic deeds of a tribe's chiefs and warriors against its many enemies. And there were tales of hunting and fishing and trapping. Some of these stories were funny; some were tragic; some were inspirational; some were educational. Yet they had one thing in common—they were all fascinating.

And there were lots of them. The Menominee, for example, had over one hundred and thirty different myths and trickster stories and magical tales of birds and animals. There were such stories as the Magic Canoe, the Miraculous Pipe, the Inexhaustible Kettle, the Singing Snowshoes, the Monster and Thunder Contest, the Fire Arrow, the Monster Killer, the Sky Lover, and many many others.

In most tribes, good storytellers were in great demand. Old people, usually men, generally told the stories. Many of these men were masters of the art of telling a good story. Seldom did their audiences go to sleep on them.

The storytelling period of most tribes was during the winter. In fact, according to the Shoshonis and some of the other tribes, some stories could not be told at other times because it might displease Old Man Coyote.

These stories were told to children both for entertainment and education, giving them instruction in the traditions and the religious beliefs of the tribe.

Among peoples who did not have a written language, as the North American Indians north of Mexico, storytelling sessions such as these were the only means of preserving their myths and legends and their tribal records—passing them on from one generation to the next by word of mouth.

Though these were the toys and games that the Indians and Eskimos played with before Europeans invaded their homeland, many Indians still play most of these games today. The influence of twentieth-century civilization can be seen, however, in the substitution of wire or steel needles (darning needles among the Chippewas) for bone or wooden pins in the ring-and-pin game, of lead for bone or horn weights in the heads of snow-snakes, of BB guns or .22 rifles for bows and arrows in shooting contests, of lead bullets for stone or wooden balls in the moccasin game, of cubical dice for two-faced wooden or bone dice (but not everywhere, as some conservatives still use the old-style dice), of rubber balls and other modern types of balls for stone or wooden balls in lacrosse and shinny.

Adolescence marked the end of Indian childhood. As soon as boys and girls were old enough, they had to start helping with the daily chores. Hopi boys helped bring in firewood and chased crows and prairie dogs out of the cornfields. At the same time, their sisters were helping their mothers carry water and were learning how to grind corn. Plains Indian girls had to go on root- and seed-gathering expeditions with their mothers and the other women of the village. And boys and girls of most tribes had to look after their younger brothers and sisters, sometimes carrying them on their backs while they themselves played games.

Though Indian youngsters may not have had to go to a regular school, they got plenty of advice and instruction on almost everything they needed to know from their older brothers and sisters, from their parents, from aunts and uncles, and from the village elders. They also learned a great deal from imitating the actions of older children and adults. And most of the time their toys and games and other recreational activities furnished good training for adult life.

By the time Indian boys had reached the age of thirteen or fourteen, or even less in some tribes, they were either making solitary fasts and vigils to acquire their guardian spirits or were taking part in warfare or raids or were undergoing other experiences that transformed them from children to adults. At about the same time, or perhaps a year or two earlier, girls were celebrating their coming of age at puberty ceremonies.

Thereafter, their childhood was at an end. But as they grew up, they would enjoy and participate in the more difficult contests and games of the adult world. And just as their fathers and mothers had done for them, they would pass along the heritage of Indian toys and games to their own children.

SUGGESTIONS FOR FURTHER READING

Bailey, C. *Tops and Whistles*. New York: Viking, 1937.

Baldwin, Gordon C. *How Indians Really Lived*. New York: G. P. Putnam's Sons, 1967.

——. *Stone Age Peoples Today*. New York: W. W. Norton & Company, Inc., 1964.

Colton, Harold S. *Hopi Kachina Dolls*. Albuquerque: University of New Mexico Press, 1949.

Culin, Stewart. *Games of the North American Indians*. Washington, D.C.: Smithsonian Institution, Twenty-fourth Annual Report of the Bureau of American Ethnology, 1907.

Dennis, Wayne. *The Hopi Child*. New York: John Wiley & Sons, Inc., 1965.

Densmore, Frances. *Chippewa Customs*. Washington, D.C.: Smithsonian Institution, Bureau of American Ethnology Bulletin 86, 1929.

Driver, Harold E. *Indians of North America*. Chicago: University of Chicago Press, 1961.

Ewers, John C. *The Blackfeet*. Norman: University of Oklahoma Press, 1958.

Feldman, Susan (ed.). *The Story Telling Stone: Myths and Tales of the American Indians*. New York: Dell, 1965.

Foley, Dan. *Toys Through the Ages*. Philadelphia and New York: Chilton Books, 1962.

Grinnell, George Bird. *By Cheyenne Campfires*. New Haven: Yale University Press, 1962.

——. *Pawnee, Blackfoot and Cheyenne*. New York: Charles Scribner's Sons, 1961.

Hilger, M. Inez. *Arapaho Child Life and its Cultural Background*. Washington, D.C.: Smithsonian Institution, Bureau of American Ethnology Bulletin 148, 1952.

Jayne, Caroline Furness. *String Figures and How to Make Them: A Study of Cat's Cradles in Many Lands.* New York: Dover Publications, Inc., 1962.

Kennedy, Michael S. (ed.). *The Assiniboines.* Norman: University of Oklahoma Press, 1961.

Lowie, Robert H. *Indians of the Plains.* New York: Natural History Press, 1963.

Marriott, Alice. *Saynday's People: The Kiowa Indians and the Stories They Tell.* Lincoln: University of Nebraska Press, 1963.

Morley, Sylvanus Griswold. *The Ancient Maya.* Stanford: Stanford University Press, revised by George W. Brainerd, 1956.

Nelson, Edward W. *The Eskimos About Bering Strait.* Washington, D.C.: Smithsonian Institution, Eighteenth Annual Report of the Bureau of American Ethnology, Part I, 1899.

Opler, Morris E. *An Apache Life-Way.* New York: Cooper Square Publishers, Inc., 1965.

————. *Childhood and Youth in Jicarilla Apache Society.* Los Angeles: The Southwest Museum, 1946.

Schultz, James Willard. *Blackfeet and Buffalo.* Norman: University of Oklahoma Press, 1962.

Stirling, Matthew W. *Indians of the Americas.* Washington, D.C.: National Geographic Society, 1955.

Underhill, Ruth. *Red Man's America.* Chicago: University of Chicago Press, 1953.

————. *Workaday Life of the Pueblos.* Lawrence, Kansas: Haskell Institute, 1946.

Wallace, Ernest, and Hoebel, E. Adamson. *The Comanches, Lords of the South Plains.* Norman: University of Oklahoma Press, 1952.

Watkins, Frances E. *Hopi Toys.* Los Angeles: Southwest Museum, Leaflet Number 19.

Wissler, Clark. *Indians of the United States.* Garden City, New York: Doubleday & Company, Inc., revised edition, 1966.

INDEX